D0599499

# POTTERYBARN
# HOME

Executive Editor
**CLAY IDE**

Style Consultant
**PATRICK PRINTY**

Editor
**SAMANTHA MOSS**

Oxmoor
House®

Oxmoor House®

Oxmoor House books are distributed by Sunset Books
80 Willow Road, Menlo Park, CA 94025

Oxmoor House and Sunset Books are divisions of
Southern Progress Corporation

SUNSET BOOKS
Vice President, General Manager  **Rich Smeby**
Vice President, Editorial Director  **Bob Doyle**
National Account Manager, Special Sales  **Brad Moses**

POTTERY BARN
President  **Laura Alber**
Senior Vice President, Creative Services,
   & Executive Editor  **Clay Ide**
Executive Vice President, Merchandising
   & Product Development  **Nancy Green**
Style Consultant  **Patrick Printy**
Print Production  **Julia Buelow Gilbert**
Editor  **Samantha Moss**
Photo Coordinator, Special Projects  **Laura Thomas**

WELDON OWEN
Chief Executive Officer  **John Owen**
President & Chief Operating Officer  **Terry Newell**
Chief Financial Officer  **Christine E. Munson**
Vice President, International Sales  **Stuart Laurence**
Vice President, Publisher  **Roger Shaw**
Creative Director  **Gaye Allen**

Senior Art Director  **Emma Boys**
Associate Publisher  **Katherine Pearson**
Managing Editor  **Laurie Wertz**
Contributing Editor  **Peter Cieply**
Business Manager  **Richard Van Oosterhout**
Designers  **Shadin Saah, Briar Levit**

Production Director  **Chris Hemesath**
Color Manager  **Teri Bell**
Photo Coordinator  **Meghan Hildebrand**

*Pottery Barn Home* was conceived and
produced by Weldon Owen Inc.
814 Montgomery Street, San Francisco, CA 94133
in collaboration with Pottery Barn
3250 Van Ness Avenue, San Francisco, CA 94109

Set in Bembo™ and Agenda™

Color separations by Mission Productions Limited, Hong Kong
Printed in Singapore by Tien Wah Press (Pte.) Ltd.

A WELDON OWEN PRODUCTION
Copyright © 2005 Weldon Owen Inc. and Pottery Barn

All rights reserved, including the right of reproduction
in whole or in part in any form.

First printed 2005
10 9 8 7 6 5 4 3 2 1

Library of Congress Control Number 2005927536
ISBN 0-8487-2765-7

# A Welcoming Home

It's been said that a person's home tells more about them than words ever could. Maybe that's because our homes allow us the unique freedom to surround ourselves with our favorite colors, textures, objects, and memories.

Over the last few decades, the shift to a more casual lifestyle has changed the way we inhabit our homes. Formally defined rooms once reserved each for a single activity have given way to versatile spaces that flow easily into one another. New advances in weather-resistant materials have extended living spaces outdoors, with decks, porches, and patios being furnished with the same comfort and style as the living room. Bathrooms have become larger, with greater emphasis on creating a spa experience. Telecommuting has made home offices more common, and affordable new entertainment technology has led to an increasing presence of media rooms in our floor plans. In the midst of all these changes, however, one truth remains the same: people are passionate about their homes.

We created this book to address the challenges we all face when we decorate our homes. The following pages include floor plans, color charts, a materials guide, and hundreds of simple style ideas that will help make decorating your home as easy, fun, and inspiring as it's supposed to be. In the interest of simplicity, we've divided the book into chapters by rooms and activities. We hope you'll discover, however, that a truly beautiful home is much more than a series of rooms. It's the ultimate expression of you and your family.

# Contents

# YOUR HOME

"MY HOME IS A VIVID REFLECTION OF WHO I AM. IT SURROUNDS ME WITH THE THINGS I LOVE MOST, AND SETS THE SCENE FOR NEW MEMORIES TO BE MADE."

For most of us, "living well" begins and ends with the private world we create for ourselves and share with friends. The homes we live in today are different in many ways from the homes we grew up in. Over the years there's been a shift away from formality and a greater emphasis on individuality, personal expression, and casual style. Gilding and grandeur are fine if you want them, and room can always be found for a fine antique, but the greatest luxury in contemporary life is

# MAKING YOUR HOUSE
# YOUR HOME

CREATING A COMFORTABLE, WELCOMING HOME THAT REFLECTS YOUR UNIQUE CHARACTER IS ONE OF LIFE'S GREATEST PLEASURES – AND ONE OF ITS GREATEST REWARDS.

without a doubt comfort – in all its guises, and in abundance. Before we can call a house a home, it must be as welcoming and soothing as it is beautiful. After all, your end goal is not merely having a striking new sofa and wall color for the living room; it is also knowing that everyone feels at home in the room. The basic elements of an appealing room are easy to identify: comfortable, well-designed seating that encourages conversation; harmony of color; lighting that meets your needs and influences your mood; beautiful things to admire and touch; and an overall sense of ease. These fundamentals of comfort remain the same throughout the entire house, from luxurious master baths or state-of-the-art home offices to well-appointed outdoor rooms. How these individual elements come together – the mix of furniture and accessories, the contrasts of texture, the use of color, the unexpected objects that give a home its character – is up to you to decide. Style depends neither on a single choice nor on a fixed set of rules; it is instead about creating a successful marriage of beauty and comfort.

Style is shaped by the way you and your family live. It is the sum of a room's many parts and possibilities, arranged to tell a distinctive, coherent story. In these pages you'll find creative decorating ideas that will help you weave your own story through every area of your home. If you work with an experienced interior designer, you can go far in breaking the rules and daring to take risks. But you don't need professional advice to create a comfortable home. You just need to

# DECORATING IS NOT ABOUT IMITATING A STYLE. IT'S ABOUT EXPRESSING YOUR OWN.

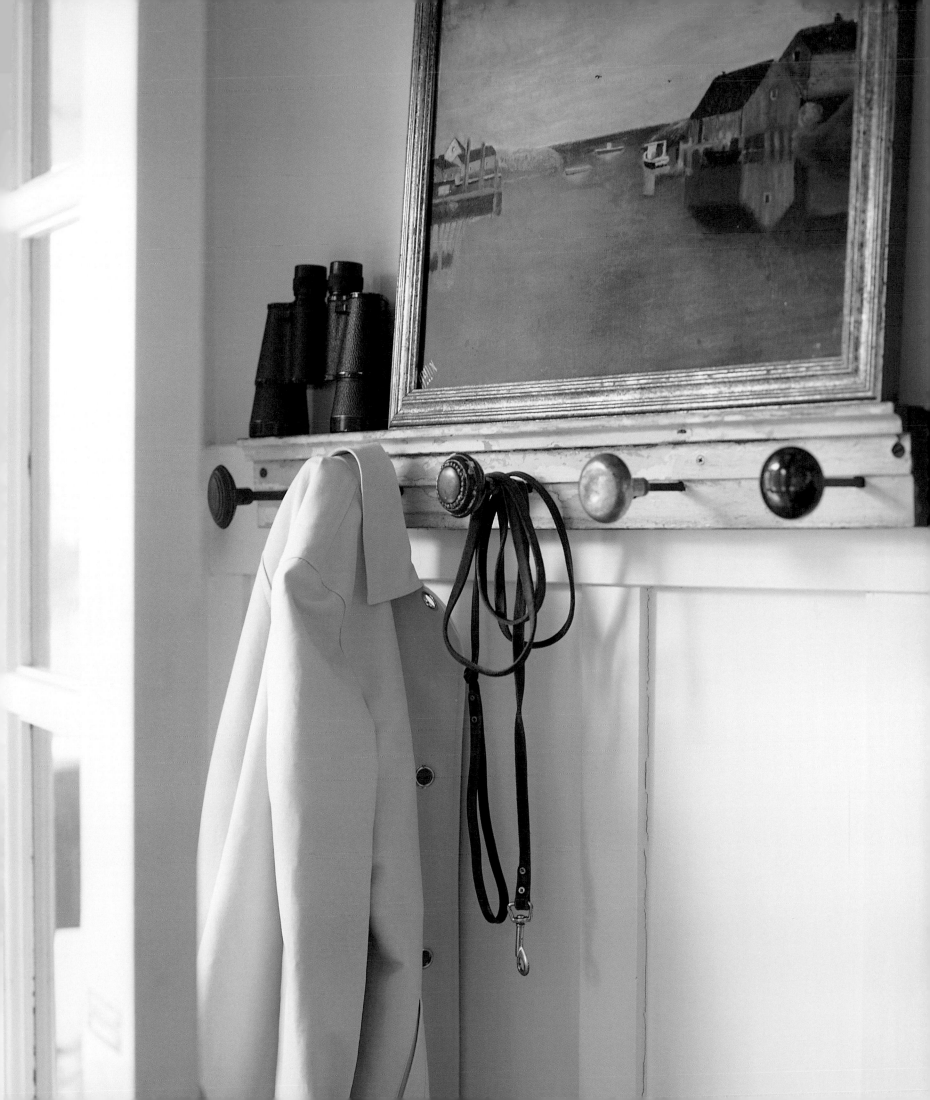

know what you love, and trust your preferences to guide you. The simplest route to identifying your style is to spend time leafing through design magazines, books, and catalogs. Take note of anything that strikes you, whether it's an entire room or just an idea for a window treatment. Clip out photos that have colors, patterns, or shapes that attract you. These clippings may also be based on intangible elements – a quality of light, the size or shape of a room, a warm mood, or memories evoked by an image. In addition to photo clippings, gather paint and fabric swatches that you like. Start a clippings folder for reference, and continue adding to it until you have three or four dozen entries. Then spread out the collection and see what's there. Is it full of warm wood or stainless steel? Do the rooms burst with color, or are you naturally drawn to off-white? Are there more sparsely furnished open spaces, or are they mostly intimate rooms filled with

# TRUE LUXURY IS ABOUT COMFORT, AND MAKING PEOPLE FEEL AT HOME.

collectibles? You'll begin to see a pattern in your choices and end up with a better sense of your innate decorating preferences. All that's necessary now is to make it happen, within budget and in your space.

Whether decorating a small apartment or a ten-room house, it's best to begin with an overall color palette that will be carried out in paint, fabrics, and furnishings and convey a style consistently throughout your home. Decorating is an ongoing, long-term process, so it's best to have something of a master plan in place, so that adjacent rooms flow smoothly from one to another. Thinking in terms of the whole house needn't be seen as restrictive, however. You can still experiment with moods – more formal in some spaces, more playful in

others. Even if you modify it later on, deciding on a color scheme for the entire house is especially helpful in this early planning stage. It will direct your efforts and spare your having to choose from among too many options. In the Color chapter of this book (page 302), you'll discover strategies for selecting a palette and making sure it extends harmoniously into all the areas of your home. Once you have your style and color preferences in mind, tackle one room at a time. If you concentrate on a single space, your efforts will pay off more quickly, and the results will be far more satisfying than if you take on too much simultaneously. This one-step-at-a-time principle also allows you to refine your style choices as you see each room take shape.

# SHARING OBJECTS AND MEMORIES THAT ARE IMPORTANT TO YOU IS THE MOST NATURAL EXPRESSION OF YOUR STYLE.

When you've chosen the space that you want to work on, sketch out a floor plan to get your ideas on paper. Throughout this book you'll find practical ideas for mapping out effective floor plans and bringing together all the varied elements that comprise a successful space. Start by establishing seating groups for conversation and areas for activities such as office work or watching movies. Look at the traffic patterns through the room and arrange furniture to accommodate smooth passage. Make a list of your lighting needs for the space and make note of possible sources of ambient, accent, and task lighting. Now is the time to consider window treatments, too, whether casual or formal, simple blinds or plush draperies. Then, with your floor plan sketched out, fill in the details by choosing furnishings and

# YOUR HOME IS AN ORGANIC, LIVING ENTITY. IT GROWS AND CHANGES JUST AS YOU DO.

accessories with an eye toward your overall style and color palette. Strive for a balance between long-term investment and affordable splurges. Part of the fun of decorating is playing with the season's new colors or trendy new patterns, but you can enjoy them in a pillow, a throw, or some other accessory instead of committing to them in a major piece of furniture. This approach satisfies a yen for something fresh while preserving a background of choices you can live with

for a long time. When investing in significant pieces, make quality, comfort, and enduring style your guides. Design trends come and go, and homes evolve over time. What remains constant is the need for comfort and the natural desire to put people at ease. Remember that what you are creating is not a showcase but a home that suits the way you live. Making your guests feel at home is less about the design of the chairs and more about the warmth of your welcome.

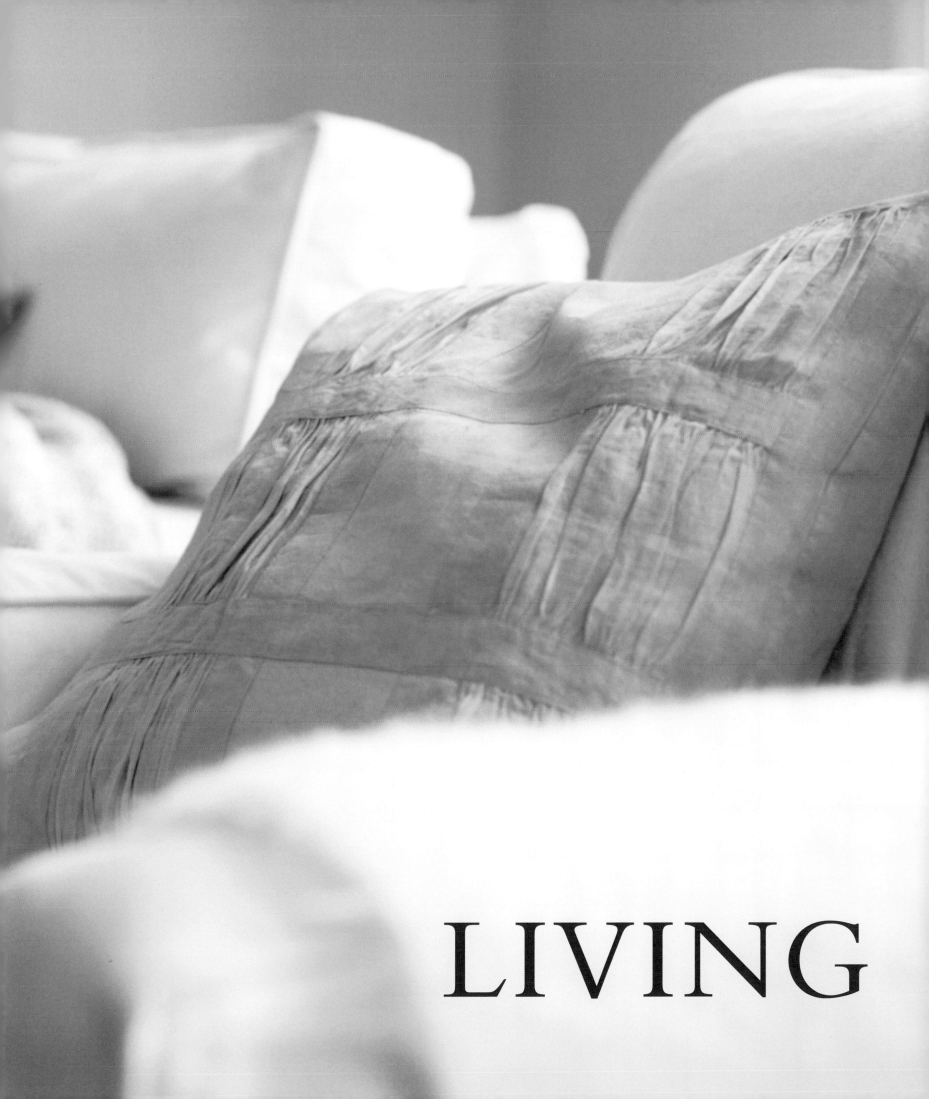

LIVING

"I WANT A ROOM FOR LIVING, A SPACE THAT REFLECTS MY STYLE AND EXPERIENCES, WHERE EVERYONE FEELS COMFORTABLE – AND THEY NEVER WANT TO LEAVE."

ELEMENTS OF A SUCCESSFUL

# LIVING SPACE

Living rooms are, simply put, just that – spaces full of life.
They're the places where we spend much of our time at
home – and a lot of our decorating energy. But living goes
on throughout the whole house, and lessons learned from
the living room apply to every area of the home. Your main
living space in many ways sets a tone for your house, so it's
important to give thought to how it influences and inspires
the decor of adjoining rooms, including outdoor spaces.
In this chapter you'll find ideas that help make living spaces
all through the house more pleasurable to spend time in.

# How to Plan a Living Space

The ultimate success of decorating any room depends upon clearly identifying your goals for the space as you begin. In your early planning, focus on functionality as well as style to arrive at an ideal arrangement.

Whether you're redecorating or simply rearranging and refreshing a room, before you start choosing colors and buying new furnishings, take time to map out the room as a whole. Draw a floor plan in a consistent scale and add furnishings in the same scale. Begin by sketching in large furnishings such as sofas, easy chairs, and armoires on your diagram. These key pieces will determine what other furnishings are needed and how you might use pieces you already have. Then, plan for traffic patterns around them. Major pathways require 36–48 inches

(90–120 cm) for comfortable passage. Allow at least 18 inches (45 cm) between a coffee table and sofa, and 24 inches (60 cm) between other pieces of furniture.

Ask yourself how the room will be used, and which additional furnishings are needed – occasional tables, ottomans, lamps, storage pieces, extra chairs, and so on. Do you want the room to be more formal or casual? Will your family use it mostly as a media center, or do you enjoy entertaining and need multiple conversation areas? Consider adding furnishings that increase the functionality of the space, such as wall shelving for storage or a table that doubles as a bar during parties. Plan for area rugs after all furnishings are in place. To anchor a seating group, a rug should be large enough for all the furniture to sit on it. If that's not possible, use a rug slightly larger than the coffee table.

## OPEN-PLAN LIVING AREA

This open-plan room (above and preceding page) has separate activity zones that are subtly differentiated while leaving ample space for traffic flow.

■ A U-SHAPED SEATING GROUP allows the greatest number of people to sit together.

■ A DIVIDING LINE between seating area and dining table is delineated by the back of the sofa.

■ THE CONVERSATION AREA is further defined by a large rug, while wood floors in the dining area are left bare.

■ OPEN PASSAGES to other rooms and to the outdoor deck are created by "floating" furniture – positioning it away from the walls – in the center of both spaces.

■ SMALLER OCCASIONAL CHAIRS used in the space offer flexibility.

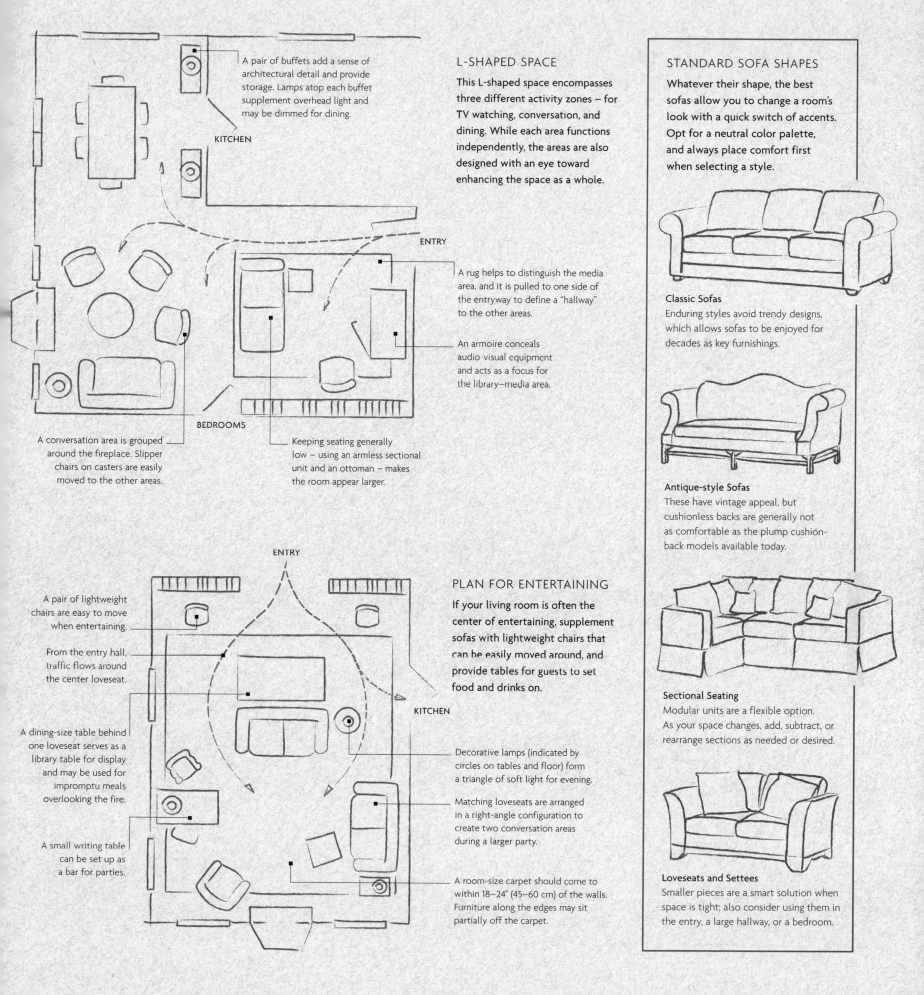

A pair of buffets add a sense of architectural detail and provide storage. Lamps atop each buffet supplement overhead light and may be dimmed for dining.

KITCHEN

## L-SHAPED SPACE

This L-shaped space encompasses three different activity zones – for TV watching, conversation, and dining. While each area functions independently, the areas are also designed with an eye toward enhancing the space as a whole.

## STANDARD SOFA SHAPES

Whatever their shape, the best sofas allow you to change a room's look with a quick switch of accents. Opt for a neutral color palette, and always place comfort first when selecting a style.

ENTRY

A rug helps to distinguish the media area, and it is pulled to one side of the entryway to define a "hallway" to the other areas.

An armoire conceals audio-visual equipment and acts as a focus for the library–media area.

### Classic Sofas
Enduring styles avoid trendy designs, which allows sofas to be enjoyed for decades as key furnishings.

BEDROOMS

A conversation area is grouped around the fireplace. Slipper chairs on casters are easily moved to the other areas.

Keeping seating generally low – using an armless sectional unit and an ottoman – makes the room appear larger.

### Antique-style Sofas
These have vintage appeal, but cushionless backs are generally not as comfortable as the plump cushion-back models available today.

ENTRY

A pair of lightweight chairs are easy to move when entertaining.

From the entry hall, traffic flows around the center loveseat.

## PLAN FOR ENTERTAINING

If your living room is often the center of entertaining, supplement sofas with lightweight chairs that can be easily moved around, and provide tables for guests to set food and drinks on.

### Sectional Seating
Modular units are a flexible option. As your space changes, add, subtract, or rearrange sections as needed or desired.

KITCHEN

A dining-size table behind one loveseat serves as a library table for display and may be used for impromptu meals overlooking the fire.

Decorative lamps (indicated by circles on tables and floor) form a triangle of soft light for evening.

Matching loveseats are arranged in a right-angle configuration to create two conversation areas during a larger party.

A small writing table can be set up as a bar for parties.

A room-size carpet should come to within 18–24" (45–60 cm) of the walls. Furniture along the edges may sit partially off the carpet.

### Loveseats and Settees
Smaller pieces are a smart solution when space is tight; also consider using them in the entry, a large hallway, or a bedroom.

Bringing together friends and family is one of life's greatest joys and privileges. Whether gathering all your loved ones or mixing old friends with new, everyone should always feel at home in your living room. Seating arrangements are the starting point. How you set up a room affects the way that people interact, so plan ahead for gatherings large and small by ensuring that there's plenty of opportunity to mingle. It's true that strangers sometimes find one another across a crowded room, but

# GATHERING
## FAMILY AND FRIENDS

SUCCESSFUL LIVING SPACES PUT EVERYONE AT EASE, STARTING WITH AN EFFECTIVE SEATING PLAN THAT INSPIRES SPONTANEITY AND INVITES EASY CONVERSATION.

most of us are more comfortable at closer range. Eye contact is key, and it should be easy to establish, whether between an intimate pairing of chairs or within a large conversation circle. Seating configurations require a logic to them, so look for a natural point of focus to provide it. If your room has a fireplace, take advantage of it and arrange a seating group around it during the cool season; a bank of windows looking out at a garden or a water view makes a perfect focal point in the summer. Make sure there's room to bring in extra seating when needed, plenty of places to set down drinks, and lots of pillows for added comfort.

# Room for Entertaining

In a space frequently used for parties, multiple seating arrangements in separate areas offer plenty of room for people to mix and mingle.

Successful entertaining is enhanced by a floor plan that eases traffic flow. Where space allows, subdivide seating areas in a large room to form smaller, more intimate groupings. This gives guests a choice of conversations to join, and lets family members use the space simultaneously for different purposes. Before a party, move nonessential pieces out of the way to give a room a more spacious feeling. Then, include lightweight, portable chairs in your seating plan to accommodate more guests and make it easier to move freely from one group to another. In smaller rooms, bring in stackable stools or floor cushions to supplement seating.

## WHY THIS ROOM WORKS

Creating three distinct areas for gatherings in this spacious living room makes it perfect for day-to-day family use as well as for entertaining a crowd.

■ AN OPEN FLOOR PLAN is inviting to large groups and encourages guests to mingle and interact.

■ MULTIPLE SEATING AREAS expand the possibilities for conversation. Two facing sofas flank the fireplace, four easy chairs encircle a coffee table, and a sheltered daybed provides a spot for a quiet chat.

■ WHITE UPHOLSTERY ties the different areas of the room together and creates a mood of serenity.

■ CASUAL WOODEN CHAIRS in singular shapes add interest and are easy for guests to move as they please.

■ AREA RUGS in a neutral color anchor the main seating groups without disrupting the unifying effect of the honey-colored pine flooring.

## WHY THIS ROOM WORKS

This room takes a traditional arrangement and gives it a casual update by incorporating informal fabrics and accent pieces.

■ **WELL-LOVED ANTIQUES** that show a little character pair with white canvas slipcovers for a casual mix.

■ **CRISP WHITE TRIM**, on the mantel and French doors, emphasizes the room's architectural details. The collection of vases on the mantel maintains the simplicity of the palette.

■ **SOOTHING BLUE WALLS** have classic appeal. The color is repeated in subtle shadings throughout the space.

■ **UNADORNED WINDOWS** allow sunlight to stream through the French doors, and mirrors and silvered surfaces reflect it, adding understated brilliance.

GATHERING FAMILY AND FRIENDS

# Classic Comfort

Enliven a traditional room with a mix of vintage and current styles, adding thoughtful accents that place comfort before formality.

The standard seating arrangement of sofa, coffee table, and a pair of chairs all grouped around a fireplace has held its popularity for good reason. It makes great use of space, puts people at ease, and can be rendered with an almost infinite selection of styles. Creative choices in color, furniture, and accessories allow you to follow a classic decorative framework but bring it up to date, making even the most traditional rooms come alive with a fresh blend of old and new.

To bring a more informal feeling to a traditionally arranged room, begin with seating that feels as good as it looks, upholstered in easy-care fabrics and accented with throw pillows. Include beautifully weathered or vintage-style pieces to give the room a lived-in look. Use lighter, more casual window treatments – cotton shades or sailcloth panels instead of heavy draperies, for example – or, leave windows bare or dress them with sheers to establish a bright, airy feeling.

# Flexible Seating

When selecting furniture for your living area, choose pieces and arrangements that can be shifted with the seasons or reconfigured for special events. Sectional seating is ideal for this purpose, but you can apply the same principles to other furniture. If you have a pair of sofas, smaller ones offer more flexibility than large ones when rearranging a floor plan; matched armchairs are more easily paired side-by-side or grouped around a table than mismatched ones. Benches and ottomans are especially adept at playing dual roles — stylish coffee tables for one event, extra seating for the next.

**A warm-weather setup**, *above*, puts the sofa in position for admiring the garden view; the grouping's focus is directed away from the fireplace. In fall and winter, *opposite page*, attention moves to the blazing hearth after a quick rearrangement of sofa and chairs.

**A quartet of armchairs**, *left*, works as an intimate variation on the classic arrangement of two sofas facing each other. This setup is ideal for an evening of board games or lively conversation.

Sectional seating is one of the most versatile systems, taking up less space than a combination of chairs and sofas. The absence of arms on many designs also contributes to a sense of openness. Systems are usually sold in units (corners plus one-armed or armless chairs, chaises, and sofas), letting you tailor seating to your situation. Armless units offer the most flexibility for rearrangement.

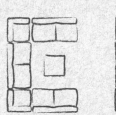

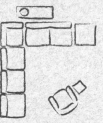

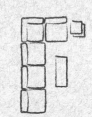

**U Arrangement**
Offering maximum seating, its scale may call for larger companion pieces like an oversize ottoman in place of a coffee table; allow 18" (45 cm) clearance.

**Corner Arrangement**
Sections of equal length should be balanced with a large-scaled chair. Instead of using a coffee table, you might use a console table behind one or both sections.

**L Arrangement**
A rectangular coffee table completes an L-shaped seating group. In a tight space, nesting tables kept at one end are a useful alternative to a coffee table.

# Fireplace Options

People are naturally drawn to fire, and a hearth is one of the most inviting focal points in a home. Due to its visual significance, a fireplace is often a room's most important structural element, too. Because a fireplace tends to dominate a room, even small changes to its mantel, surround, or hearth can have a big impact.

If your existing fireplace is less than perfect, all is not lost. Often the surface elements and scale can be improved (see below) without changing the firebox or chimney, which are more complicated projects. Ideally, a fireplace's style and scale should match the room's architecture and should be as accessible and inviting as possible. Consider whether you want a deep mantel or a shallow one, a colorful inner surround of tile or stone or something more subdued. Luxurious materials like marble and granite add luster to fireplace surrounds, mantels, and hearths, and using them in such a small area yields a great effect at a relatively modest cost.

**A Rumford fireplace**, *right*, is an 18th-century design that features a high opening and a shallow firebox to project radiant heat. A tall, vertical firebox matches the scale of rooms with high ceilings.

## DESIGN LESSON GIVE YOUR FIREPLACE A NEW LOOK

mantel

surround of noncombustible material

firebox

hearth

Should you find yourself faced with an oddly proportioned or deteriorated fireplace, look first at simple ways to update its appearance. Several intermediate measures, from painting or resurfacing to installing a new mantel, can improve the look of an old fireplace for a fraction of what a complete replacement might cost. The materials listed at right are available at most home repair and fireplace stores.

Depending upon your home repair skills, it may be wiser to hire a carpenter or tile setter to do the work for you rather than try to tackle it yourself. Firebox structural repairs should always be done by a professional.

■ CLEANING SOLUTIONS for hearths and stone remove soot and smoke stains.

■ FRESH PAINT offers the quickest and most affordable way to give dated or unattractive brick fireplaces a new look.

■ NEW MANTELS vary greatly in style, from custom-cut marble or limestone to prefabricated wood or stone, cement, "cast-stone," or even iron versions. Most home centers and lumber yards carry a range of models, including antique reproductions.

■ REPLACEMENT SURROUNDS, whether fashioned from stone slabs cut to size or made of ceramic or stone tiles, can usually be applied directly to existing surfaces, or the surfaces can be replastered with stucco.

## Corner Hearth

Where wall space is at a premium, building a fireplace into a corner is an attractive option that lends a cozy mood to any room. Seating groups oriented toward a corner position bring fresh dimension to a room, and benches along one or both sides of a fireplace make it even more inviting.

## Traditional Wood

Wooden mantels were historically made in the architectural style of the house, and you should aim for the same compatibility. With salvaged mantels and reproductions available in Arts and Crafts, Federal, Victorian, American Country, and many other styles, it's easy to find a mantel that reflects your home's character.

## Flush Mantel

A shallow or flush mantel is an ideal choice for a smaller room. This slender moulding of faux stone adds architectural detail without overpowering the room or occupying too much space. It extends out from the wall just enough to gracefully frame the opening and support a painting on its ledge.

## Raised Hearth

A hearth that sits about 18" (45 cm) above the floor puts the fire at a height where it is more easily seen from anywhere in the room. It also simplifies the task of starting and maintaining a fire. The hearth can be extended to either side to create a low bench for fireside seating.

## Antique Stone

This small-scale iron fireplace with marble mantelpiece was originally designed to burn coal but has been converted for contemporary use. Its beautifully incised surround, arched firebox, and simple mantel need no further embellishment. Reproductions of antique surrounds and mantels are widely available.

## Hole-in-the-Wall

This minimalist approach defines a current trend in fireplace design that's become popular in contemporary homes. Another example of a fireplace style that evolves from architecture, the hole-in-the-wall fireplace generally features a horizontal firebox, positioned low on the wall, with no mantel or surround.

MANTEL DISPLAYS SET A TONE FOR A LIVING ROOM. ALLOW YOUR FAVORITE COLLECTIONS TO TAKE CENTER STAGE.

**A Federal-style mirror**, *top left*, is given eclectic companions in this asymmetrical composition. The objects are united by a black, tan, and white color scheme. Choose pieces that repeat basic forms (the balls echo the round mirror), then adjust your arrangement until you've achieved a pleasing balance.

**A cinephile's collection**, *left*, pairs vintage movie posters with a row of antique cameras and equipment for a witty homage to cinema history.

**A natural theme**, *above*, unifies this display. The repetition of round and rectangular shapes gives a sense of rhythm and movement to the grouping, drawing the eye from the shells to the flowers, then up to the unusually framed book hung on the wall above.

**A group of magnifying glasses**, *right*, is mixed with black-and-white pottery pieces for a whimsical display. The grouping creates a dynamic lineup of shapes brought together by a common color palette.

The trend of having an open-plan family space has become increasingly common in today's homes. It's easy to see why. Perhaps nothing enhances family life as much as a room that's generous enough for everyone to occupy together, and well-designed enough for them to do it harmoniously. The trick to making an open space work is balancing a desire for some degree of separation with a need for overall harmony. Begin by zoning the room for different activities – reading, movie

# PLANNING A
# SHARED SPACE

WITH SO MANY FAMILIES TRADING FORMAL LIVING AND DINING ROOMS FOR AN ALL-PURPOSE "GREAT ROOM," A SHARED OPEN SPACE IS BECOMING THE NEW HEART OF THE HOME.

watching, dining, and so on. This helps establish a sense of having intimate areas within the larger space. Signal transitions from one activity zone to another with area rugs and strategic furniture groupings. Unify the space by sticking to a single cohesive style, and use just one or two principal colors throughout to minimize visual clutter. Choose materials, finishes, and fabrics that stand up well to constant use, furniture that's generously scaled, and multiple sources of both ambient and task lighting. Give special attention to display, and allow plenty of space for storage – an especially important element here, where so many activities are at play.

PLANNING A SHARED SPACE

## WHY THIS ROOM WORKS

This handsome space displays a family's taste for both culture and comfort. Its classic lines are softened by casual furnishings.

■ A WARM NEUTRAL PALETTE of white, cream, and tan is an elegant backdrop for unfussy furnishings and accessories.

■ A BABY GRAND PIANO sets the tone for the decor; its rich color is echoed in a refined Federal mirror, black accents, and warm wood pieces.

■ A PLUSH SHAG RUG adds texture to the subdued color scheme and invites visitors to get comfortable.

■ CLUB CHAIRS in soft brown leather balance the formality of the decor.

■ CASUAL PHOTOS framed in silver are displayed with honor on the piano.

# A Well-Mannered Family Room

Music and games are part of the household routine in a refined family room whose comfortable style gets dressed for company.

Sometimes you need a room that's designed for quiet grownup gatherings and leisure time at the piano, but you also need space for family get-togethers and game playing. An understated decorative scheme is the best solution for a refined and easygoing family space.

Comfort and elegance combine beautifully in a room whose palette is drawn from muted neutrals and earth tones. Neutrals are always the most flexible backdrop, as the look of a room can be freshened quickly with a change of accents. Warm neutrals convey a low-key luxury that's easy to dress up or down: curl up with the kids at play and the dogs at your feet, then host a cocktail party later that evening. Temper a room's formality with decidedly informal furnishings such as leather easy chairs and a casual wool pile rug, and keep accessories simple and graphic.

# Zoning Strategies

Give shape to an open-plan room with subtle dividing lines that preserve its openness while creating discrete areas for all of its uses.

The challenge of an open floor plan is finding ways to define zones for different activities – or different family members – while maintaining a luxurious sense of space. Creating visual divisions between zones is usually the best strategy. Facing a sectional sofa away from the rest of an open room can demarcate seating, dining, or work areas. Partial walls, bookcases, folding screens, and portières (fabric draperies used as screens) are also effective room dividers; by stopping short of the ceiling, they preserve a room's openness. Zones can also be delineated by a change in flooring materials or a difference in ceiling heights.

As a general rule, a few large-scale pieces of furniture make a greater impact in an open space than a lineup of smaller pieces, which can create a disorderly look. Sectional pieces or flexible pairs are practical choices because they help to define activity areas and are easily rearranged as your needs change.

## WHY THIS ROOM WORKS

Designed for a family with young children, this open space uses imaginative visual divisions to establish distinct zones for relaxing, playing, dining, and cooking.

■ A NEUTRAL PALETTE of white and taupe unifies the room's different areas. Bursts of red and grace notes of ebony add vitality and contrast.

■ A GENEROUS BUILT-IN SOFA defines a comfortable TV-watching area and visually separates the crafts workspace tucked behind it. Suspended red lampshades emphasize the distinction between living and dining areas.

■ A PARTITION WALL screens a kitchen work zone from view and establishes the bold red accent color that's used throughout the room.

■ CHILD-FRIENDLY FABRICS and scuff-proof floors make this a space where kids are welcome to play freely. The blackboard coffee table on wheels can be moved to other areas of the room. A unique wheeled dining table is expandable, allowing it to be adjusted or moved to accommodate groups of different sizes.

# Family-Friendly Living

When the whole family shares a small space, every inch counts. Closed cabinetry and portable containers keep things tidy.

Small spaces need smart planning, and that's especially true when several family members all need a place to pursue their work or creative interests within one room. Keeping everyone's equipment, playthings, books, and art supplies organized and easily accessible requires a variety of tailor-made storage solutions.

Bins on wheels make it easy for kids to cart toys or art supplies to where they're needed. Assigning each child his or her own storage bin helps keep belongings orderly and encourages pride of ownership; it also makes kids more likely to pitch in at cleanup time. Utilize the space under a coffee table to hold baskets of books and toys where children can reach them. Adults' more expensive "toys," like audio and video equipment, are best housed behind doors that can be firmly shut, so closed cabinetry is their perfect home.

## WHY THIS ROOM WORKS

This family room keeps storage for kids' belongings within their reach at floor level, while the parents' workstation and audiovisual equipment remain better protected.

- **FLOOR-TO-CEILING CABINETS** conceal a television and other electronic equipment when not in use, and offer off-season storage space above.

- **ROLLING BINS** and stackable toy caddies allow for quick cleanups. Baskets of children's books are stowed beneath a sturdy coffee table.

- **AN OLD-STYLE SCHOOL DESK** gives kids workspace, where they can do artwork and still be near the family.

- **OPEN SHELVING** creates a home-office workstation and gives adults easy access to supplies and equipment.

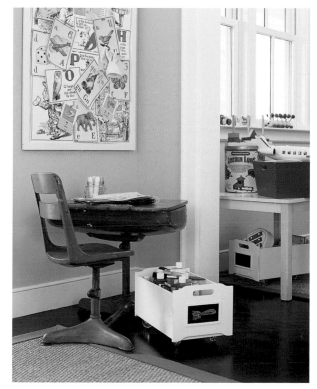

# Shelving Options

Bookshelves are among the most efficient of storage options. They also add architectural interest to a room and allow great opportunities for creative expression, displaying not only book collections, but also family mementos, photographs, and artwork.

Shelving should be consistent with a room's overall decorative scheme. Wood is the most common choice because it can be stained or painted to match the existing trim; metal shelves give a more contemporary look. For a clean fit, align edges and tops of shelves with doors, windows, or other architectural elements in the same visual plane. Well-designed bookcases have consistent spacing of vertical supports, and ideally horizontal shelves are positioned in one continuous line for the length of the unit (though shelf heights may vary to hold diverse objects, electronic equipment, or large books). Plan to have the largest openings at the bottom, to avoid a top-heavy or skewed appearance.

**Wraparound bookshelves**, *right,* turn a corner of an open-plan room into a reading nook with deep windowsills and a handsome display shelf at ceiling height. Extending shelves across the tops of the windows gives the unit a tailored look.

## DESIGN LESSON ORGANIZING BOOKS ON SHELVES

Once you have your bookshelves in place, it's time to put them to work. You might not think of filling shelves as a design decision, but a well-planned arrangement that mixes books with favorite objects makes an attractive display that's easy to access. Bookshelf displays are an intimate revelation of the soul of the family. Books and mementos announce areas of particular interest, favorite authors and artists, and memorable family trips. If you'd like to reorganize your shelves, for a more handsome display or simply to make it easier to find particular books, here are some guidelines that will turn your wall of storage into a handsome room decoration as well.

■ TAKE STOCK of what you need to shelve. Remove everything and sort it by size or genre, so you can see what you've got to work with.

■ LEAVE SPACES within the upright books for placing objects or collections, or to hang artwork on the wall or bookcase back. This essentially creates display cases within the shelves, which lightens the overall look of the bookcases.

■ ARRANGE BOOKS BY SIZE: The most visually pleasing arrangements place the larger books and objects on the bottom shelves and smaller items up higher. As you fill shelves, allow 1–2" (3–5 cm) clearance above each row of books.

■ ADD CONTAINERS to hold loose items and maintain an orderly look. Use baskets or storage boxes for photos, maps, and letters.

## Uniform Cubes

Wall-to-wall shelves composed of uniformly sized cubes reduce the span between vertical supports — one way to minimize sagging of the shelves over time. The orderly grid also works well for displays of books and diverse objects.

## Freestanding

A trio of 12"-deep (30 cm) bookcases transforms a stair landing into a mini-library and still leaves plenty of room for foot traffic. Lined up flush along a wall, freestanding bookcases mimic the look of costlier built-ins.

## Fireplace Framing

The walls on either side of a fireplace are a natural location for shelving. In this configuration, the top shelf extends across the fireplace, unifying the entire wall and forming a frame for displaying artwork above the mantel. Leaving the top shelf empty gives it a more tailored look.

## Space Efficient

All you need for bookshelves is a depth of 12" (30 cm), and that can be found in the most unexpected places around your home. Under-window shelving makes the most of unused space, creating a surface for displays or a base for window seating.

## Wraparound

Over-the-door shelving has long been popular with book lovers short on space, and it also adds architectural interest. When shelving uprights frame a door or window, they make it appear to be recessed.

## Painted Background

Paint the wall behind your shelving a deep contrasting color to call attention to decorative objects interspersed among the ranks of books. In floor-to-ceiling bookcases, varying the vertical spacing between shelves within the grid creates a more dynamic arrangement.

**LIVING WITH BOOKS** IS AN EVERYDAY PLEASURE. CREATIVE DISPLAYS LET YOU SHOW OFF FAVORITE TITLES THAT REVEAL A BIT ABOUT WHO YOU ARE.

**A long shadow box**, *above*, turns a stack of books into a witty display. The box is filled with a colorful collection of pulp-fiction paperbacks, and its back is lined with enlargements of pages from the books, a clever personal touch that gives the arrangement a finished look.

**Paper-wrapped books**, *right*, form a sleek and slightly tongue-in-cheek arrangement, stacked and topped with favorite objects. White paper harmonizes disparate dust jackets, and handwritten titles on the spines give them a casual, personalized appearance.

**A row of cookbooks**, *opposite top*, is kept tidy and made more decorative by a collection of vintage graters, used to separate groups of titles. Equally suited to the task would be cloth bags of rice or flour, vintage food tins with period labels, wooden cutting boards, or other collections of culinary objects.

**A bookstore-style arrangement**, *opposite bottom*, places a handful of titles face out, a setup that varies a bookcase's visual grid and invites guests to browse. Change the display to highlight different titles or to feature a recently read favorite.

There was a time when a proper living room was arranged like a stage set and decorated to demonstrate a family's standing in the world. Reserved for special occasions, a living room required formal behavior. The new living room, though, is all about comfort, and goes a step beyond welcoming family and friends in style. It should be a place where you feel equally at home taking an afternoon nap or hosting a cocktail party, and a place where your children want to bring friends home

# PROVIDING COMFORT

WHEN A GUEST SLIPS OFF HER SHOES AND CURLS UP ON YOUR SOFA LIKE A CONTENTED CAT, TAKE IT AS A COMPLIMENT. YOU'VE SERVED UP THE GREATEST LUXURY: TRUE COMFORT.

to play. Comfort means putting people at ease, both physically and emotionally. The ingredients are simple: commodious furnishings, soft textures, and thoughtful touches that invite guests to relax. It's about flattering light, a plump pillow for a friend to press into the crook of his back or rest behind his neck, and extra chairs for last-minute guests. It's the touch of soft leather, the spring of a pile rug, the scent of fresh flowers. Add the flicker of candlelight, an embroidered pillow, and a soft throw to toss over bare feet, and you're there. True comfort comes from being surrounded by loved ones and enjoying the beauty of home.

Warm jewel tones, candlelight, and sensuous materials add luxurious accents to an informal living room that anyone can feel at home in.

■ CASUAL SLIPCOVERS, paired with pillows and throws in sumptuous fabrics, strike a perfect balance between laid-back and elegant.

■ ANTIQUE AND NEW PIECES are mixed for a relaxed mood.

■ WARM CHOCOLATE WALLS create a cocoon-like feeling. Earth tones, even in deep shades, can work as neutrals in a sophisticated palette like this one.

■ BAMBOO SHADES are a more informal choice than draperies.

■ A WOOL RUG introduces pattern to the room, adding depth to the decor.

PROVIDING COMFORT

# A Textural Blend

A soothing haven for family and friends layers on comfort in the form of deeply textured fabrics, warm colors, and luxurious accents.

Your home can look elegant and sophisticated and still be inviting and comfortable. The secret lies in giving rooms an appealing textural mix – combining furnishings and accents to create spaces that are stylish but that still put everyone at ease.

Keep the mood easy and uncomplicated by layering basic furniture pieces with fabrics that reward the senses, such as a plush shawl or throw tossed over the back of a sofa. Rich wall colors, leather, wood, and soft lamplight all contribute depth and warmth to a space. At nightfall, candlelight casts a warm glow.

A combination of casual and luxurious fabrics keeps a room looking polished but feeling comfortable. Dress up cotton slipcovers with pillows and throws of supple leather, suede, or velvet. Cotton velvet, damask, and chenille are all lush-looking fabrics that have the added benefit of easy care. Quilted, tufted, or ruched fabrics also heighten a room's sense of luxury.

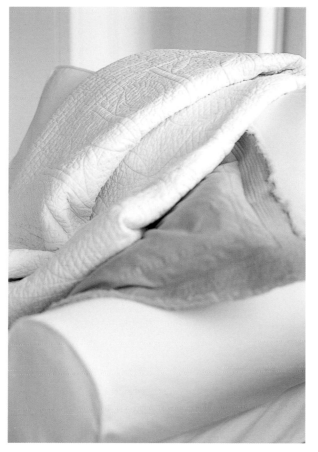

# A Restful Palette

To create a room as restorative as an old-time summer hotel, keep the colors and furnishings simple and maximize natural light.

Comfort comes in many forms, but few things are as soothing as daylight playing across a palette of serene colors. Rooms with a subdued color scheme have a calming effect, especially when furnishings are soft and understated and accent hues are reserved.

In an all-white room, variations in texture are essential for variety. Wood paneling, rustic antiques, natural woven rugs, wicker furniture, quilted linens, and flowers and botanicals all add textural interest. If privacy is not an issue, leave windows bare to let in daylight, and enjoy the interplay with nature. Outdoor furniture, such as rattan or wicker pieces, can be fitted with comfortable cushions, lending natural style to a room.

## WHY THIS ROOM WORKS

Solarium-quality light gives this room a rare serenity and freshness, with just enough contrast to engage the eye and plenty of cool green to soothe it.

■ GENEROUS SEATING makes this a welcoming space, whether you're hosting a whole crowd or looking for a spot to snooze.

■ AN ALL-WHITE COLOR PALETTE, accented with a range of greens, changes with the shifting light throughout the day.

■ NATURAL TEXTURES, from the wicker chairs and sisal rug to the worn woods and soft fabrics, add interest to the monochromatic color scheme.

■ ABUNDANT GREENERY in flower arrangements and potted topiaries brings the outdoors in.

■ IMPROMPTU ACCENTS reinforce a casual air. A whimsically framed botanical print on the mantel is surrounded by garden clippings.

Once you've created an inviting living area inside your home, extend what you love about the room outdoors to your yard or patio. Increasingly, home-loving nesters view the near outdoors not as a separate realm but as a natural extension of the home. In keeping with a desire for a more casual lifestyle, relaxing and entertaining out-of-doors has become more prevalent because it requires less fuss and planning than it does indoors, plus it's easier to include children in the festivities. And

# EXTENDING
# OUTDOORS

OUR HOMES ARE OPENING UP TO EMBRACE THE OUTDOORS AS NEVER BEFORE. THE CHERISHED OLD PORCH, PATIO, AND TERRACE HAVE BECOME THE NEW LIVING ROOM.

with all the water-resistant furnishings and fabrics now widely available, you can decorate your deck or patio with the same sense of style and forethought that you use indoors. Entryways, too, are enjoying new attention. What once was just a way in and out of the house is now being treated with the same respect and care as other rooms. Once you get outdoors, it's now easier to stay there longer – especially in regions where the climate is temperate for much of the year. Thanks to sleek space heaters, canopied terraces, fire pits, and outdoor fireplaces, everyone can enjoy the yard, deck, patio, or porch as their year-round retreat.

Surrounded by lush plantings and flooded with air and light, this gracious patio offers all the best of indoor-outdoor living.

■ A DEEP PERGOLA with climbing bougainvillea vines affords filtered shade by day and provides a sense of enclosure.

■ WEATHERPROOF CHAIRS fitted with water-resistant fabric cushions are the outdoor equivalent of indoor easy chairs.

■ MULTIPLE FRENCH DOORS run the length of the patio, blurring the line between indoors and out and providing easy access to interior rooms and food and supplies.

■ A FREESTANDING BAR can be brought indoors and used off-season.

EXTENDING OUTDOORS

# An Easy Transition

The best outdoor spaces blur the boundaries between house and yard and marry beautiful surroundings with indoor amenities.

One of the many pleasures of an outdoor room is the sense of being partly in nature, partly sheltered from it. To heighten this feeling, make the transition from indoors to out as seamless as possible. Arrange furniture groupings as you would indoors, and define the edges of the exterior space with a change of paving or a shift from paving to lawn or gravel. Clear views and easy access between inside and out – large French doors are ideal – are key in creating a sense of flow.

Choose furniture made of teak or other moisture-resistant woods that can be left outside to slowly weather to a silver-gray. Use plump cushions and fabrics that are both water- and mold-resistant for lasting wear. Any lighting that you add should be subtle; supplement it with soft candlelight, using windproof hurricane lamps or oversized lanterns. Setting up an outdoor bar or serving table cuts down on trips to the kitchen, letting you spend more time with guests.

## WHY THIS ROOM WORKS

Informal seating plus an abundance
of creature comforts give this
covered porch the appeal of an
old-fashioned summer camp.

■ **THE STONE FIREPLACE** allows the
porch to be used in cooler seasons
and provides a dramatic focal point.

■ **SAILCLOTH DRAPERIES** form a
moveable "wall" that helps protect
the room from rain and wind.

■ **LIGHTWEIGHT SEATING** – seagrass
wing chairs and iron folding stools –
is capacious yet easily transported
indoors or to winter storage.

■ **WEATHERPROOF MATERIALS** like teak
and zinc improve with age and use.

■ **ELECTRICAL OUTLETS** in the floor
make sufficient lamp lighting possible.

EXTENDING OUTDOORS

# Inside-Out Living

A stone fireplace transforms a breezy summer
porch into a year-round gathering place for
open-air relaxation and enjoyment.

A covered porch has always been more than just a
pleasant place to pass the time. Sheltered porches are
like treehouses for adults, with a special aura that
softens the poignancy of summer's end. A trend toward
including outdoor fireplaces on porches, decks, and
patios, however, now makes it possible to extend the
outdoor living season long past summer's end. Just as in
a traditional living room, a fireplace provides a natural
focal point around which to build an outdoor room.

Especially if you enjoy a seasonally dry climate, you
have more options in outdoor furnishings. Furniture
made of rustproof metals or moisture-resistant hardwoods such as teak, redwood, and nyatoh can be
supplemented with lightweight, portable furnishings
and accent pieces from indoors. Rugs, colorful throws,
extra pillows, and even reading lamps make it more
enjoyable to settle in. For a greater sense of enclosure,
hang draperies made from all-weather fabric.

# Inviting Entryways

Entryways offer a first impression of your home, so it's especially important to consider their dual nature when decorating them. As a practical matter, entryways are about comings and goings, so you need a smart system for managing clutter in one of the home's smallest rooms. On an emotional level, entries are about being welcomed and celebrated, so you'll want to include thoughtful touches that make arrivals feel like an event.

Making it all work begins with storage that brings order to the space. If your entryway has no closet, hang hooks on the walls for coats and hats, and provide bins or baskets for wet boots and umbrellas. Designate a place to set packages, mail, and keys, such as on a hall table or credenza. A chair or bench to sit and remove shoes is also a thoughtful addition. To visually link the entry to the rest of the house, use furnishings, colors, and decorative accents that are similar to the adjoining rooms. And don't forget to lay out a welcome mat!

**A sturdy sideboard**, *right*, provides a hardworking storage system for a busy household entryway. Extra containers for larger items leave a clear path for coming-and-going traffic, and wall hooks turn a row of hats into a decorative yet practical display.

## DESIGN LESSON CHOOSING FLOORING FOR ENTRYWAYS

Whether your door opens into a foyer or directly onto the main living space, an entryway's flooring takes a lot of wear. It also has to make a positive first impression. The kind of flooring you choose helps to establish not only the tone of the entryway but also of the rest of your house.

Dual concerns influence the choice of materials here: formality and wearability. An elegant style of decor or a formal house exterior might call for a dignified introduction. Similarly, casual interiors should be announced by an informal entryway. You can make a foyer seem bigger than it actually is by using the same flooring in it as the rooms it adjoins. This may mean sacrificing durability in the hall for appearance in the adjoining rooms, if you choose wood instead of tile, for instance.

■ WOOD, *top left*, is warm, beautiful, and smooth underfoot but requires periodic refinishing and protection in wet weather.

■ PORCELAIN TILE, *top right*, is made from a special mix of clays and minerals that can be fired at an extremely high temperature, yielding a hard, dense tile that resists stains and scratches. Large-format porcelain tiles are often designed to look like stone.

■ TEXTURED STONE, *bottom left*, is a versatile option that complements a wide range of styles. It adds instant luxury and stands up well to everyday use.

■ TERRA-COTTA TILE, *bottom right*, offers a warm, rustic look. Because it's unglazed, it requires sealing but is otherwise easy-care.

## Painted Wood Gate

A front gate should be inviting while reflecting the style of the house behind it. This cheerful carved wooden gate echoes the rustic style of the rammed-earth house just beyond. Open panels are a friendly touch, making the gate less imposing, and its bright color keeps it festive.

## Grill Gate

Transparency makes a sturdy gate seem less imposing and more welcoming. This beautiful scrolled wrought-iron gate, which invites visitors to peek down the garden walk, is a repurposed vintage window, as strong as it is beautiful. Its dramatic style heightens the pleasure of arrival.

## Staircase Entry

Make the most of an older house's stair-dominated entrance by highlighting architectural details with glossy paint and laying down a stair runner, to add interest and lead the eye upward. This "runner" is cleverly painted onto the stairs, leading the eye to a stack of vintage suitcases that doubles as off-season storage.

## Living Room Entry

When a front door opens directly into a living room, define an "entry" with a large piece of furniture such as a console table or cupboard. Hooks placed high on the wall turn coats and other belongings into an artful display. A drawer conceals the keys, gloves, scarves, and mail that often accumulate.

## Mudroom

Rustic bunkhouse style suits a weekend retreat or might be used in the garage or utility entrance of a busy household. Personalized "carrels" are labeled with blackboards, making it easy for everyone to find their hats, boots, and rain gear on the way out — and to put them back in place on the way in.

## Half-Wall

Open rooms need a transitional space, too. Where no defined entry to a room exists, create a sense of a foyer with a freestanding unit like this high-backed bench. It gives people a place to sit and take off boots or muddy shoes, has a handy storage compartment within its bench, and hides an area behind it that's used for storing outdoor gear.

The display of things that are personally meaningful is among the most democratic of art forms, and one of the most engaging. What is comforting to family is often fascinating to guests, and what we respond to most in a room is personal expression. Put on view the artwork, photos, and objects that you love – creatively using shelving, mantels, table surfaces, and wall spaces – and let them tell a story about your interests, heritage, and travels. Special pieces and collections are among the

# SHOWCASING
# FAVORITE THINGS

DISPLAYS OF TREASURED ITEMS AND PERSONAL COLLECTIONS BRING LIFE TO A HOME. OFFER GUESTS A GLIMPSE INTO YOUR PASSIONS WITH ARTISTIC ARRANGEMENTS IN EVERY ROOM.

most important elements of your home, and though there's no rule about what to include, a few guidelines will help you show your personal favorites to best advantage. Arrange objects and photos for maximum impact, grouped by color, material, shape, or theme; arrangements in groups of three or five are especially pleasing to the eye. Framed photos of your ancestors, the family farm, and your parents as newlyweds posing in front of their first car take on the poetic sweep of a genealogical chart when seen marching up a stairwell wall. Even antique postcards become a unique gallery when matted, framed, and proudly displayed.

# Shelves for Display

Wall-to-wall shelves are a dramatic showcase for books, singular objects, and collections. Plan ahead for the most effective display.

Few decorating tricks are as transformative as installing a wall of shelves to put books, decorative objects, and art on view. Whether freestanding or built-in, shelving is ideal for displays because it contains clutter, is space-efficient, and can be changed and updated easily.

Vary the height of individual niches to accommodate different-sized items, and mix groups of books, favorite accessories, and found objects in creative ways to add interest. (If favorite things also happen to make clever bookends, all the better.) Painting shelves a uniform color ensures a clean appearance; a contrasting color on the back wall makes objects stand out. Accent lighting adds drama; if possible, plan ahead for electrical outlets.

## WHY THIS ROOM WORKS

Built-in shelves devoted to art and family treasures animate this room, give it a warm character, and establish order.

■ STRONG HORIZONTALS at table height and at the top of the shelving establish a bold framework for the shelving's grid and highlight the upper tier, which houses a single collection.

■ A QUIET PALETTE allows treasures to stand out against the light gray background; objects on the shelves seem to come forward visually.

■ LARGER LOWER SHELVES for oversize books are practical and important for visual balance.

■ A PAIR OF LARGER OPENINGS within the grid lend symmetry and create space for displays of artwork.

■ ANTIQUES AND FOUND OBJECTS interspersed among the books provide variety and interest.

■ CADDIES for loose change and mail make practical use of whimsical objects.

GROUPING YOUR COLLECTIONS IS A SURE WAY TO CREATE DISPLAYS WITH DRAMA. USE REPETITION OF FORM, COLOR, AND THEME AS POWERFUL UNIFIERS.

**Antique teacups**, *above*, and other small, fragile collectibles tend to get lost in a large cabinet. These wall-mounted display cubes show off each item to advantage and create a bold pattern against a dark blue wall.

**A collection of natural objects**, *right*, have greater visual interest when one is given prominence. Here, a delicate ostrich egg is highlighted on a display stand, providing a focal point for the grouping.

**An assortment of keys**, *opposite top*, read as a collection when displayed with purpose. The backdrop here is a magnetic bulletin board fitted with rectangular magnets, from which the keys dangle on simple ribbons.

**A row of antique weights**, *opposite bottom*, gains presence when arranged on a slightly raised tray. This beautiful composition is capped by a colorful accent – a single sprig of bittersweet.

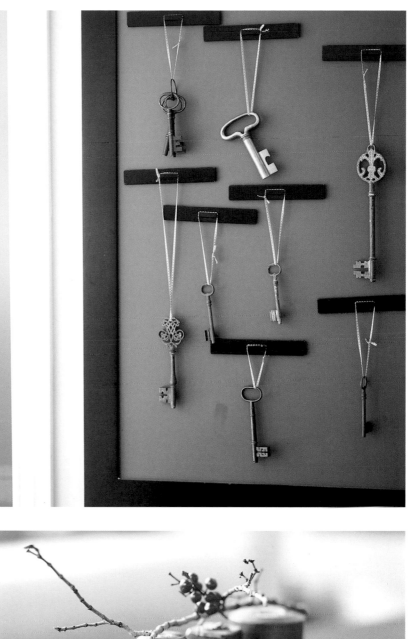

# A Home Gallery

Make a bold statement with a wall devoted to a gallery-style display of photographs, ready to change at a moment's notice.

Well-displayed photos can transform a room, whether they're signed works you've collected or prints from your most recent outing with the digital camera. Not only are photographs one of the more affordable forms of art, they also lend themselves to a variety of display styles. If you're working with your own photographs, the options for display are greater still, since you can control the size and cropping of the prints as well.

Instead of hanging framed photos on a wall with nails or tacks, try propping them on narrow shelves. Using shelves makes it easy to rearrange or add new pieces to your gallery. Arrange photos asymmetrically to give the display a sense of dynamism and possibility.

## WHY THIS ROOM WORKS

Careful pacing of color and a sense of restrained luxury make this space surprisingly warm. White walls and furnishings keep the focus on the photo collection.

■ NARROW-LEDGE SHELVES visually recede into the white background but offer plenty of space for an ever-changing gallery. A ceiling-mounted display light illuminates the collection at night.

■ UNFRAMED PHOTOS hang from wire with clips, allowing for quick changes to vary the display's visual pacing.

■ SIMPLE FRAMES in similar styles and colors give the disparate photographs a sense of unity.

■ LOW-PROFILE FURNISHINGS let the colorful photo display take prominence in the space.

■ CAREFULLY CHOSEN ACCESSORIES pick up the strong colors in the photographs and extend them into the room.

HANGING PHOTOGRAPHS IS AN ART UNTO ITSELF. FRAME, MAT, AND GROUP IMAGES FOR GREATEST IMPACT, AND FIND UNEXPECTED PLACES TO HANG THEM.

**Photos in various sizes**, *opposite top*, are arranged asymmetrically and mixed with mirrors and collected objects to form an attractive composition. Harmony is maintained by using only black-and-white images and a consistent color for all frames. Weaving mementos into your photo display is a compelling way to tell a story.

**Black-and-white photos**, *opposite bottom*, have a surprising freshness when mounted in a series on the doors of a glossy black cupboard. The collection is uniformly framed in red with identical white mats. Look beyond your four walls to find interesting places to display photographs — perhaps lined up on the floor leaning against a wall, or resting on ascending shelves mounted along a stairway.

**Precisely aligned botanical photos**, *left*, bring gallery-style polish to this display. When grouping photographs in a grid, it's usually best to stick to a single subject or theme and to choose either all black-and-white images or all color. Frames in a grid arrangement often look best when they're identical, though mat size may vary to fit the individual photos. Measure carefully to ensure that you have the same amount of space between frames for a uniform grid.

**Panoramic photographs**, *above*, are highlighted by unique placement — beneath a window ledge — intensifying their impact and telling a compelling story in black and white. Arranged in a horizontal row, the pictures allow a narrative to unfold, much like flipping through the pages of a book.

# DINING

"I LOVE SHARING FOOD WITH FAMILY AND FRIENDS. I WANT EVERYONE TO FEEL AT HOME IN MY DINING ROOM, FREE TO TALK AND LAUGH FOR HOURS AROUND MY TABLE."

# DINING SPACE

Of all the rooms in the house, the dining room is the one that has seen the fewest changes in our lifetimes – at least in terms of basic furnishings and setup. What has changed is our style of dining. Where formal rooms and fancy place settings were once the norm, we now enjoy relaxed elegance in open-plan spaces, take meals at the kitchen island or in an open courtyard, and use a dining area as a home base that welcomes activity outside of mealtimes. Our dining spaces are also warmer and more personal than ever before.

The rooms on the following pages illustrate just a few of the options available for creating livable dining spaces indoors and out, and making them a highlight of your home.

# How to Plan a Dining Space

The dining room is by nature a simple space, but it can lend itself to spirited styling. After all, its main function is celebration. Look for quality and comfort in a dining set, then add furnishings that suit your entertaining style.

The centerpiece of any dining space is its table. Wood remains the most common choice, and is popular for its warm patina and easy care. Rich wood finishes suit almost any decorating style, while painted tables tend to be more informal. The surprise of black painted wood freshens a dining space and, like the classic little black dress, it can be informal or sophisticated as the occasion warrants. The style of dining chairs is another key element in creating a distinctive personality for the room. They should gracefully complement the table, though

they need not match it (see pages 98–99 for helpful advice on selecting dining chairs). It's an advantage to have storage for dinnerware located right in your dining room, whether built-in or freestanding. A buffet is an efficient option that does double duty as a storage piece and serving table. A taller glass-door cabinet or hutch is attractive beccause it adds height in a room where the furniture tends to be low.

This is a room of primarily hard surfaces, so bring in fabrics to soften and warm the space. Drape the table in crisp linens or casual runners that let the beauty of the wood show through. Hang curtains or fabric shades at the windows. Drapery panels of velvet or silk catch candlelight beautifully, adding texture, warmth, and a sense of luxury. Upholstered chairs or slipcovers offer other ways to introduce color, pattern, and texture.

### CASUAL DINING ROOM

Comfortably furnished with an oval table and armchairs, this room (above and preceding page) invites everyone to settle in for an enjoyable meal.

■ ROUND AND OVAL TABLES are becoming increasingly popular because they naturally stimulate conversation, allowing each person to see and hear all other diners.

■ UPHOLSTERED ARMCHAIRS encourage guests to linger after meals.

■ A WINE CABINET adds character to a dining space. It's also an efficient storage component, with a surface that can be used for buffet service and an upper cabinet that holds glassware and dinnerware as well as displays of collections and objects.

■ A HANDSOME CHANDELIER suggests a festive occasion without the formality of an ornate crystal fixture.

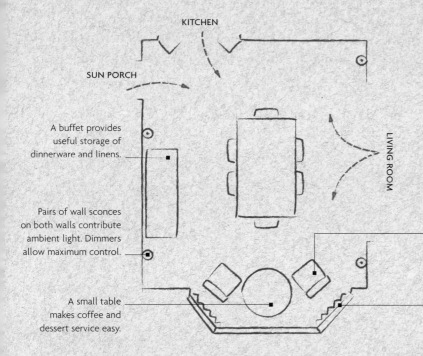

KITCHEN

SUN PORCH

LIVING ROOM

A buffet provides useful storage of dinnerware and linens.

Pairs of wall sconces on both walls contribute ambient light. Dimmers allow maximum control.

A small table makes coffee and dessert service easy.

## CLASSIC DINING ROOM

Several doorways open onto this traditional floor plan, but a 4' (1.2 m) passageway prevents congestion. The dining table sits 3' (90 cm) away from furniture along the walls to allow space for guests to slide their chairs back.

Two extra chairs flank a small side table; when leaves are added to the dining table, these are easily pulled to the main dining area.

Draperies in the bay window bring soft texture and warmth to the space.

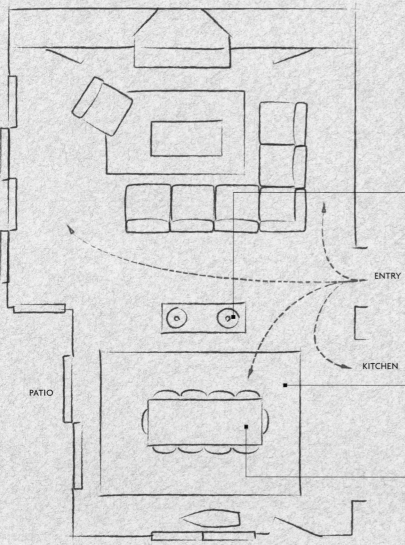

ENTRY

KITCHEN

PATIO

## OPEN-PLAN DINING AREA

This dining area sits between the living area and the kitchen (at bottom right, not shown). Sliding glass doors on one wall lead to an outdoor patio, so traffic through the room was a main consideration in furniture arrangement.

A console table topped by lamps separates the dining space from the living area. It offers convenient storage for dinnerware and a surface for serving buffet dinners, snacks, and drinks.

A large rug helps define the dining area within the open plan. It is 36" (90 cm) larger than the table on all sides, so it allows chairs to be pulled in and out at the table while still remaining on the rug.

The dining table seats ten people with extra leaves inserted.

## HOW MANY PEOPLE CAN YOUR TABLE SEAT?

To prevent diners from bumping elbows with each other, allow at least 24" (60 cm) of table space for each person.

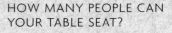
24" (60 cm)

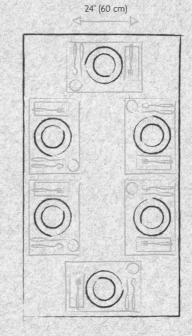

**Rectangular Table**
72 x 32–36" (180 x 81–90 cm) seats 6
90 x 32–36" (229 x 81–90 cm) seats 8
108 x 32–36" (274 x 81–90 cm) seats 10
120 x 32–36" (305 x 81–90 cm) seats 12

See page 99 to determine how large a table your dining area can accommodate.

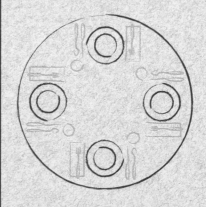

**Round or Oval Table**
A pedestal base offers more flexible seating, allowing you to fit more people.

Round 45" diameter (114 cm) seats 4
Oval 66 x 45" (168 x 114 cm) seats 6
Oval 73 x 45" (185 x 114 cm) seats 6–8

The formal dining room that many of us grew up with is like a three-piece suit: handsome, traditional, and fairly formal. Today's dining rooms are more like an outfit you'd wear on casual Friday. Comfort is key, and beauty comes from a stylish combination of informal elements. While the classic furniture pieces remain, they are now more comfortable, functional, and in keeping with the style of the rest of your home. You don't even need to have a separate formal room. Carve a dining

# REDEFINING THE
# DINING ROOM

TODAY'S DINING SPACES ARE RELAXED AND CASUAL, WITH FORMAL TOUCHES COMING FROM WELL-CHOSEN ACCESSORIES AND PLACE SETTINGS RATHER THAN FROM THE ROOM ITSELF.

area out of open space, set up in an extra room, or embrace an open-plan kitchen/dining layout. Furnish your room with unconventional pieces, mismatched chairs, and favorite objects. Store dishware, flatware, and linens on open shelves in eye-catching vignettes. For a swept-clean look, hang cabinets with glass panes on the wall, or stow tableware in a generous armoire. Extend a warm welcome by using casual table dressings like place mats, chargers, or runners instead of formal linens, and use colorful slipcovers and cushions on the chairs. Hang family photos or artwork on the walls, and find every opportunity to give the space your personal stamp.

# The New Formal Dining Room

If you love to entertain but your dining room is too small, take advantage of an underused parlor to create a spacious dining area.

Some older homes have an extra parlor that sees little use because residents gravitate toward a larger den or family room. If you have such a space and your formal dining room can't accommodate as many guests as you'd like, why not move your dining table into the extra room? Not only are these rooms frequently larger, they also often have architectural details that make dining more luxurious. Fireplaces add instant warmth, and mantels offer a convenient surface for setting out candles and floral displays. Built-in bookshelves let you showcase personal collections or decorative dishware, making the room feel welcoming.

## WHY THIS ROOM WORKS

This former parlor is now a dining area with luxurious seating, ample space, and classic appeal. A simple change of accents dresses the room up or down for fireside suppers or formal dinner parties.

■ A MAHOGANY BUFFET is fitted for wine storage and offers a surface for wine and cheese service. Decanted bottles of wine hold cheese menus, indicating types that are well suited to the particular vintages.

■ LINEN TABLE RUNNERS suggest a special occasion without the formality of a full tablecloth. They also expose the beauty of the bare wood.

■ LEATHER ARMCHAIRS contrast with linen slipcovered chairs and convey a warm, clublike atmosphere.

■ A LUSH CENTERPIECE adds a sense of abundance that belies its simplicity. It's made from a simple mass of tulips.

■ MANTEL AND SHELVES display art, family photos, and collected objects, personalizing the dining space.

# Open-Plan Dining

Wide-open living offers limitless opportunities for creative entertaining. Carve out a dining area, then add warm, welcoming accents.

If you live in an open-plan space, you have the unique opportunity to create "rooms" in your home right where you want them. Without four walls to form a dining room, you can designate one instead with a well-planned arrangement of furnishings.

Laying down a rug is the simplest way to define a dining area within which to arrange your table and chairs. Make sure the rug size is generous enough so that chairs can be pushed back without slipping off. Furniture for storing dinnerware and linens can also be enlisted to further anchor the space. For example, a bar, buffet, or sideboard might be used to form another "wall" between the dining and living areas.

## WHY THIS ROOM WORKS

Dressed in rich colors and warm textures, this dining area in the corner of an open loft has all the comfort and graciousness of a more traditional dining room.

■ A SIDEBOARD BAR at one end of the room helps to define the space. The mirrored wall is a pleasant contrast to the brick and maintains the area's openness.

■ A MIX OF TEXTURES provides visual and tactile interest and makes this a sumptuous place to dine: a paisley throw used as a tablecloth, natural linen slipcovers with pleated hems, a patterned rug, and gleaming tableware.

■ BUILT-IN SHELVES installed behind openings in the brick wall serve as an open "butler's pantry" and form an artful display wall.

■ TABLEWARE is attractively stored in and easily accessed from the neat storage and display area. Bundled place settings of flatware make short work of laying the table.

## WHY THIS ROOM WORKS

This contemporary dining room still has the traditional table, chairs, and buffet but also reflects the owner's strong eye for unique design.

■ AN OPEN BUFFET offers an opportunity to show off a collection of vintage silver and keeps pieces within reach for use when entertaining.

■ GALLERY-STYLE FRAMED PHOTOS give the walls character and visual interest without cluttering the space.

■ A NATURAL THEME pulls the room together. Fig branches serve as a centerpiece, and aspen leaves are a repeated motif on the linen napkins. An abaca rug keeps the mood casual.

■ A GRAPHIC TABLE COVERING is a copy-shop enlargement of a leaf image, protected by Plexiglas.

REDEFINING THE DINING ROOM

# A Fresh Take on Classic Style

It's time to update the definition of "classic." Give a time-honored setup a new twist by taking a contemporary approach to design.

The traditional recipe for dining room furnishing calls for a table for six or eight plus a buffet or hutch. This recipe doesn't specify what the pieces must look like, however, or how they ought to be dressed. Reinterpret the formula using your own fresh approach, and bring up-to-the-moment appeal to the classic setup.

Some people save their favorite things to display in other parts of the house, but decorative items are more than welcome in a dining room, where they can be appreciated throughout the course of a meal. Display collections of silver or servingware, and use the walls as a gallery to hang rows of photographs or artwork. Keep the table simple, with modest settings and a striking centerpiece. Mix delicate antique pieces with strong contemporary styles — hotel silver with simple white dinnerware, for example.

# Lighting Options

The basics of lighting in the dining room are simple: indirect light is always better than direct; illumination from lamps and candles should flatter guests; and flexibility is key. Design a versatile lighting plan so that light can be adjusted for time of day or occasion.

A mix of indirect ambient and direct task lighting is best for the table, where you often may be doing more than just dining. Chandeliers are most common for dining room ambient lighting. Pendant fixtures, recessed downlights, or wall-mounted gallery lights can provide a blend of both ambient and task light. Dimmer switches offer extra control and flexibility. Accent lighting adds drama: use picture lights or spotlights to highlight art, objects, or architectural features, and make generous use of candlelight for atmosphere.

Whatever the mix of lighting, the styles you choose convey tone. For example, votive candles create a casual mood, while tapers suggest a more formal occasion.

**A properly hung chandelier**, *right*, casts light onto the table without shining into diners' eyes. It should be scaled to the size of the table and should never obstruct views across it.

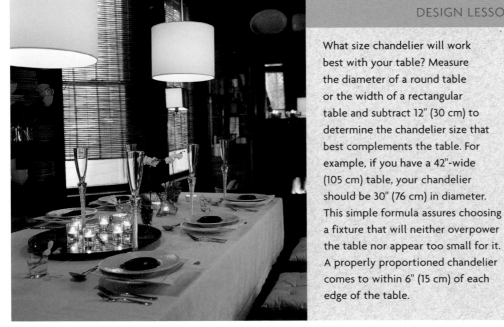

## DESIGN LESSON PLANNING FOR CHANDELIERS

What size chandelier will work best with your table? Measure the diameter of a round table or the width of a rectangular table and subtract 12" (30 cm) to determine the chandelier size that best complements the table. For example, if you have a 42"-wide (105 cm) table, your chandelier should be 30" (76 cm) in diameter. This simple formula assures choosing a fixture that will neither overpower the table nor appear too small for it. A properly proportioned chandelier comes to within 6" (15 cm) of each edge of the table.

**How to hang a chandelier**

If you have 8' (2.4 m) ceilings, the bottom of the chandelier should be 30" (76 cm) above the tabletop. If your ceilings are higher than 8', raise the chandelier 3" (8 cm) for every extra foot (30 cm) of height. The chandelier should be centered on the table, even if the electrical connection in the ceiling is not. Use a length of decorative chain to carry the wiring to the chandelier, which should be hung from a secure hook over the table center.

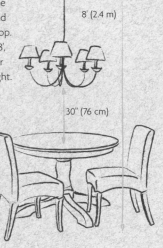

8' (2.4 m)

30" (76 cm)

**Pendant Lights**, *right*
Hanging pendants shed ample direct light over this kitchen work surface and breakfast bar. Because opaque shades don't throw light over a large area, multiple lights are necessary to cover an expansive space.

**Table Lamps**, *far right*
Balanced light is essential in a dining room, to illuminate its perimeter as well as the table. Wall sconces traditionally provide lighting for a buffet but can be difficult or expensive to install. Table lamps, set on side tables and wired with dimmers, are an attractive and versatile alternative.

**Pillar Candles**, *right*
This ring chandelier holds pillar candles in varying sizes and offers an unusual, informal overhead lighting option. Similar chandeliers are available in electric versions that mimic the look of candlelight.

**Chandelier**, *far right*
A chandelier can be fanciful or tailored; the choice depends more on your style than on a generalized prescription. Once reserved only for grand dining rooms, chandeliers are now often used in family dining areas, too. Often, a room will require supplemental lighting; use recessed downlights, sconces, or table lamps.

### Wooden Chairs

All-purpose wood chairs are available in a wide range of styles. The type of wood and finish influences the formality of the room, with painted wooden chairs being perhaps the most informal. Seat cushions provide additional comfort and bring style to the decor through color and pattern.

### Armchairs

These comfortable chairs encourage lingering at the table, inviting you to sit back, rest your arms, and settle in for coffee and dessert. Armchairs are often used at either end of the table for the hosts but can be used for all seating. The key to using armchairs is making sure that the arms clear the bottom edge of the table.

### Slipcovered

Fabric slipcovers provide another opportunity to introduce pattern and color into a room of hard surfaces. Slipcovers also give a dining space great flexibility. They can be swapped out seasonally, changed to suit a formal or informal occasion, and are easily removed for cleaning.

### Upholstered

Chairs covered in fabric or supple leather are a traditional choice for comfort and afford a polished appearance. They work with almost any decorating scheme, whether formal or casual. Many chairs are covered in easy-care fabrics, and leathers are made more durable and stain-resistant now, so it's easy to maintain their patina.

### Stacking Chairs

Lightweight portable chairs are among the most convenient styles to use. They transition effortlessly between casual gatherings and sit-down dinners, and are easy to store in multiples or move around a room. Stacking chairs add a contemporary accent to a traditional dining space.

### Traditional Styles

Classic American styles like Windsor (shown here), ladderback, and Hitchcock bring a traditional note to a dining space. The curvaceous lines of Windsor chairs visually soften the geometry of a rectangular table; the simple design of a ladderback chair adds height to a sleek dining table; and the petite scale of Hitchcock chairs make them a versatile choice.

# Seating Options

The best dining rooms are as comfortable as they are visually appealing. To arrive at the best and most relaxed seating arrangement, begin with a spacious table that works well for a variety of tasks, including dining and working, then look for chairs scaled to the size of your dining space. To ensure comfortable seating and adequate elbow room around the table, allow at least 24 inches (60 cm) of space for each person.

While a matched table and chairs give a cohesive look, mixing contemporary with antique styles – or pairing a wooden table with slipcovered, wicker, painted, or leather chairs – affords you the opportunity to show some personal flair. The options for mixing and matching are unlimited, but make sure there is room to slide chairs in and out from the table easily, and note that the position of a table's legs affects how many chairs will fit comfortably. A pedestal-base table allows for more flexible seating than a table with legs.

**Long, cushioned benches**, *left*, are an unexpected stand-in for traditional dining room chairs. White-painted wooden chairs at either end of the pleasingly scuffed table round out the seating plan, giving this room a relaxed, informal feeling.

## DESIGN LESSON WHAT SIZE DINING TABLE?

How large a dining table will your room accommodate? It's easy to calculate the best size for your space. Just base it upon the room's dimensions.

### Measuring for a Dining Table

Draw a floor plan to indicate the length and width of the room and any doors and windows that affect furniture placement. Designate a spot for a buffet or other cabinetry, usually 24" (60 cm) deep. Determine how people will pass through the room and, working from the walls inward, block out 4' (1.2 m) for traffic. Allow at least 3' (90 cm) of space from all walls and furniture to pull chairs in and out easily. The space that remains in the center tells you how much room you have for a table.

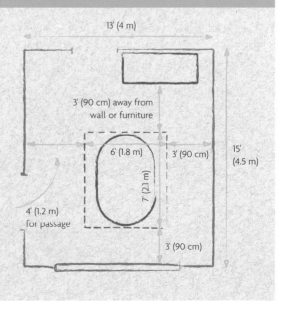

13' (4 m)

3' (90 cm) away from wall or furniture

6' (1.8 m)

7' (2.1 m)

3' (90 cm)

15' (4.5 m)

4' (1.2 m) for passage

3' (90 cm)

The secret to enjoying entertaining – and to doing it successfully – is learning to make it easy on yourself. When you've developed a system for making parties go smoothly, it allows for more spontaneity than if you have to reinvent things each time. It also makes it more likely that you'll want to entertain more frequently. The most important thing to remember is that your aim is to make guests feel celebrated, and that doesn't require much time or travail. Focus on the details that create a

# ENTERTAINING
## WITH STYLE

CLOSE FRIENDS, DELICIOUS FOOD, AND BEAUTIFUL SURROUNDINGS ARE ESSENTIAL TO A CELEBRATION, BUT THOUGHTFUL DETAILS AND CREATIVE TOUCHES GIVE A PARTY ITS STYLE.

memorable party. This is the time to bring out the hotel silver and linen tablecloths, or to dress the table with bright fabrics and colorful flowers. Make the room glow with decorative candles or lanterns, and stemware that adds reflective dazzle. Simple touches like handwritten menu cards or festive party favors placed at each setting signal the beginning of a memorable occasion. Cleverly personalized settings bring touches of whimsy to the table – place cards fashioned from photos, luggage tags, or mini chalkboards, and napkin rings made from beads, buttons, or strands of grasses. Your inventive creations are the touches that add distinctive style to your parties.

# Dramatic Practicality

The best entertaining spaces deftly combine drama with good planning and make it easy to host elegant dinners and festive parties.

If you have a lot of things you need to store, sometimes the best solution is to put them all on display. Storage as display is not a new idea, but it can work especially well in a dining space, where many pieces are so shapely and appealing that they create naturally dramatic displays. For day-to-day use, some people also keep a table set at all times, to encourage the family to sit down together instead of eating in front of the TV.

A wall of floor-to-ceiling shelves filled with tableware, stemware, and flatware makes a striking decorative statement. It's also highly practical, since items are kept within reach during parties. Set up a bar in an area out of the flow of traffic, and outfit it with an ample supply of stemware, highball glasses, cordials, decanters, and cocktail napkins. And always consider lighting: a balanced mix of ambient, task, and decorative accent lighting is key for a glowing nighttime dinner party.

## WHY THIS ROOM WORKS

The combination of casual furniture, formal table settings, and dramatic displays gives this dining room an urbane sophistication.

■ **BLACK WALLS** signal a theatricality suitable to an entertaining space. The black backdrop puts glassware, white dinnerware, and silver in high relief.

■ **CHALKBOARD PAINT** on a section of wall lets the host announce the menu.

■ **A MIRRORED BAR CABINET** continues the storage-as-display theme and adds luster to the setting.

■ **LIGHTING AT EVERY LEVEL** includes pendant lights set on a dimmer, recessed lights in the shelving and the Victorian breakfront bar, and votives on the table. Reflective accessories enhance the flickering candlelight.

This open room with its soaring vistas makes a wonderful location for entertaining, offering plenty of space for food and beverage setups and room to mix and mingle.

■ THE BUFFET TABLE is set in the open and allows access from either side, so it can serve a large group efficiently.

■ A SELF-SERVICE BAR is set apart from the buffet table on a sturdy built-in bookcase, out of the flow of traffic.

■ COMFORTABLE SEATING is arranged throughout the room and out on the porch. Generous armchairs and a sofa flank the fireplace.

■ DINING PLATES are set at one end of the table and flatware at the other, to ensure smooth traffic flow.

■ BUNDLED SILVERWARE is easier than separate pieces to carry from the table to a comfortable seat. Lash bundles together with a decorative tie.

■ MINIATURE PLAYING CARDS, tied with a loop of twine, help guests keep track of which wine glass is theirs.

ENTERTAINING WITH STYLE

# Buffet Style

Buffet-style dining is one of the easiest ways to entertain a crowd. The key to success lies in arranging the room to ease traffic flow.

Nearly everyone has occasions when they want to invite more guests than they have room for at their dining table. The simplest solution is to set up a buffet in the largest space in your house — it doesn't have to be in the dining room. A long, wide table is always the best choice, especially when dressed simply to allow plenty of room for food and serving pieces. Make sure there's space around the table for guests to move comfortably. If possible, situate the table so that guests can help themselves to food from both sides. Arrange seating groups throughout the space to encourage mingling, pulling in chairs from other rooms as necessary, and provide small tables to set down drinks.

# A Festive Scene

With a little ingenuity, you can host a large-scale dinner at home. All it takes is a creative approach to seating and a fun sense of style.

It may seem daunting to plan a large formal dinner, but it's possible to stylishly seat and serve a crowd with ease. Look for places in your home that could be turned into a temporary dining room – perhaps one end of the living room, or a wide hallway. To seat a large group comfortably, you obviously need a long table. A couple of good options are using multiple tables lined up and dressed as one, or renting banquet tables. Or forgo a single table altogether and set up a number of small tables instead, to evoke the lighthearted atmosphere of a bistro. Borrow lightweight wooden chairs from other rooms and mix them in with your dining chairs, or rent the number you need to provide ample seating.

## WHY THIS ROOM WORKS

A generous banquet table is fashioned from several square tables lined up, spanning the width of the room without crowding it. Because the table is narrow, this setup takes up less space than you might think.

■ MIX-AND-MATCH CHAIRS provide sufficient seating while establishing a casual atmosphere.

■ A SEPARATE DESSERT AREA is set up in the adjoining study to encourage guests to mingle after the main meal.

■ SPECIAL TOUCHES greet guests from the moment they arrive. Murano glass cherries adorn the menus, and gift totes are tied to chairs. Portrait "place cards" are snapshots taken as guests arrive. Splits of champagne, served in their own ice buckets with a straw, add a playful note.

■ CASUAL DECOR keeps the mood light for the festivities. A raw linen tablecloth signals informality, as do the loose and garlanded carnations used here in abundance.

FLOWERS FOR THE TABLE ARE EASY TO STYLE WHEN YOU LET A SHAPELY CONTAINER PROVIDE THE INSPIRATION, AND KEEP THE CHOICE OF BLOSSOMS SIMPLE.

A small creamer, *above left*, holds a single blossom, and one is put at each place setting. Floral arrangements don't need to be set in the middle of the table. This kind of individual centerpiece is a nice way to make guests feel special. Here the display also serves as a place card, with the guest's name written directly on the container. After the party, everyone can take their arrangement home.

Paper bags, *left,* are anything but prosaic when painted in a variety of bold colors. The bags make charming covers for an eclectic array of containers. Each is filled with a generous bunch of the same type of flower, and the painted bags complement the flowers' hues without overwhelming them.

A long, narrow vase, *above*, showcases the sweet simplicity of tulips. The white ceramic vase is low by design, adding colorful elegance to a dining table without obstructing guests' views. It's also a stylish choice for a mantel or sideboard display. For dramatic impact with minimal effort, choose just a single variety of flower to fill a vase.

Showy alliums, *right,* standing in tall glass containers make simple but striking centerpieces that add dramatic impact to the setting. To add color high and low, rest a few allium blooms directly on the table. Here, glass pebbles, normally used as vase fillers, are massed on the tablecloth to create the effect of a luminous runner.

One of the most iconic and enduring images of home is that of the whole family gathered around a table, laughing and chatting while tucking into a lovingly prepared meal. It's not surprising, then, that the most popular gathering spot in many homes is the dining table. This is the stage on which everyday life is played out and reviewed, and one of the few places in our busy world where we can catch up with one another, pass time, and celebrate events large and small. Whether you

# SETTING THE
# FAMILY TABLE

THE DINING AREA IS OFTEN A HOUSE'S HOME BASE. MAKE IT A PLACE THAT SUITS YOUR NEEDS AND REFLECTS YOUR INTERESTS, AND IT WILL APPEAL TO FAMILY AND FRIENDS ALIKE.

have a compact eat-in kitchen or a grand open-plan room, make sure that your dining area suits your family, reflects its style and interests, and can comfortably accommodate everything from holiday gatherings to game playing and bill paying. Hardwearing furnishings are a smart choice here. Choose durable furniture and tableware that can be easily dressed up for celebrations. Give the room the honor it deserves by decorating it with the things that you and your family love, adding personality and warmth with collections and artwork. Change table settings and accents often to keep the space feeling fresh and in step with the seasons.

# Seasonal Celebrations

When family and friends gather around the table, set a festive tone with colorful, easy-to-do decorations and coordinated accents.

Setting a special dinner table for an extended-family celebration doesn't require a formal setup or unusual effort. Just look to the season's bounty for inspired decorating ideas. Start with place settings in white or neutral tones, which make a perfect backdrop for napkins, tablecloths, and stemware in seasonal colors.

Whether using the earthy hues of harvest time or the soft colors of spring, you can arrange centerpieces drawn from Nature's palette. Make loose seasonal arrangements of flowers, herbs, gourds, berries, or branches. Candles are always welcome, and a single piece of stemware at each place lends just the right amount of elegance to a special occasion.

Dressed for a holiday feast, this table takes its cues from fall colors at their peak. The table setting is simple, but the colorful accents and thoughtful decorative touches make this a celebration.

■ BASIC WHITE DINNERWARE offers great flexibility for changing table decor. Mixed with accent pieces, it keeps any palette fresh and inviting.

■ A SEASONAL CENTERPIECE of pumpkins and bittersweet branches is paired with clusters of pillar candles. The natural decorations are repeated on the buffet hutch.

■ A CHILDREN'S TABLE makes little ones feel special. Kids can sit down to their own version of the grownups' table, complete with durable deep-dish plates, white sketchpads for place mats, and a supply of crayons.

■ CREATIVE PLACE CARDS encourage conversation and conviviality, especially when they involve an after-dinner game or activity.

WHY THIS ROOM WORKS

This combination kitchen–dining area is an ideal home base for gatherings throughout the day. Its cozy decor invites family and guests to take a seat and stay a while.

■ **BENCH SEATING** recalls the pleasures of eating outdoors around a picnic table – a convenient seating option for children, who can slide in and out quickly. Wicker chairs dress up the set.

■ **A WHITE DINING SET**, along with a fresh color palette and an abundance of natural accents and greenery, keep the space feeling light, open, and connected to the garden just outside.

■ **DISPLAYS OF FAMILY COLLECTIONS** engage the eye at every level, giving pride of place to favorite mementos and artwork.

SETTING THE FAMILY TABLE

# Home Base

An informal eat-in kitchen decorated with casual style makes everyone feel at ease and welcome to linger at any time of day.

An eat-in kitchen has a special appeal for family and friends alike. It's convenient for families because while Mom and Dad are preparing dinner, kids can finish up homework (and ask for help) before it's time to set the table. It's great for casual entertaining, too, since guests gravitate toward a kitchen anyway, and there's plenty of room for them to relax and chat with the cook.

One approach to decorating an eat-in kitchen is to make it as homey and cozy as possible. Give its decor the same level of attention that you would a "proper" dining room, but take advantage of its informality by making it more personal. Signal that this is "family central" with displays of favorite objects and mementos that invite comment and recollection. Set collections and family treasures – groupings of collectible pottery, an array of children's artwork, beach shells from a summer outing, souvenirs from family trips – around the space to give it character and interest.

# Storage Options

Your enjoyment of your dinnerware and serving pieces will last only as long as they retain their beauty, and that means making sure they get proper care and handling. You don't need to develop a whole new regimen, however. Just follow some basic commonsense storage rules, and your dishes, stemware, flatware, and serving pieces will stay beautiful for generations.

Whether you choose to display your treasures out in the open for easy access and dramatic style, or tucked away in cabinets for a streamlined look, the first consideration is adequate protection. The fragile surfaces of many dinnerware pieces require plenty of space to protect them from friction, and adequate wrapping or storage systems that ensure safekeeping. Items that see daily use such as flatware, crockery, and sturdy glassware are best kept close at hand and can be stored more casually. Finer pieces like china, crystal, stemware, and silver call for special consideration.

**A wall of open shelves**, *right*, turns this hallway into a modern version of a butler's pantry. Adjustable shelves accommodate pieces of varying heights, and some are fitted with baskets for holding linens and flatware. Baskets on high shelves hold less-used items.

## DESIGN LESSON CARING FOR DINNERWARE

When the big celebration is over and it's time to put away your special serving pieces, linens, and flatware, some special rules apply for the storage of pieces you don't use frequently.

Padded, zippered cases made for safekeeping fine china are available in various sizes. You can make your own storage boxes, lined with bubble wrap and divided into sections with cardboard, to hold odd-shaped items like gravy boats and terrines; be sure to use acid-free archival cardboard. Felt and foam are proven materials for protecting stacks of china. Dish protectors in various sizes are commercially available to insert between plates; you can also cut your own felt or Styrofoam dividers to slide between dishes.

- **FINE CHINA** should be washed by hand with a mild detergent (without bleach or lemon scent) before storage, and, if unused, should be taken out and washed annually. Never stack plates higher than 8" (20 cm).

- **FINE LINENS** should be laid flat, wrapped in acid-free paper, and rolled rather than folded, to prevent mold and permanent creases.

- **SILVER PIECES** are best kept in drawers or boxes lined with special tarnish-preventing fabric, or wrapped in acid-free tissue (never in plastic wrap, wool, felt, newspaper, or chamois) and stored in polyethelyne bags.

- **CRYSTAL AND STEMWARE** should be washed by hand in warm water with mild detergent. Store upright on shelves or in padded cases.

**Shelf Storage**, *far left*
A series of shallow shelves, adjusted to allow for the height of the glasses plus about 1" (3 cm), make glasses easy to reach. Always place crystal stemware upright when stored on shelves.

**Hanging Stemware**, *left*
Wineglasses and stemware must be stored with care. Hanging wineglasses by their stems in a mounted rack helps keep the bowls free of dust.

**Covered Displays**
Neatly arranged rows of glassware, plates, and teacups become lovely additions to a room's decor when stored in china cabinets or wall cabinets with glass doors. On-view storage is appealing because so many dining essentials have beautiful shapes. What's more, built-in cabinets can be customized to fit unusual serving pieces.

**Open Displays**
"Floating" display shelves mounted over a sideboard keep everyday dining necessities close at hand for daily use, and make buffet-style service simple for larger gatherings. Add one or two mementos to your mix of dinnerware and glasses, and your storage solution doubles as an attractive dining room display.

**Silverware**, *right*
Place settings slipped into individual tarnish-proof fabric pockets, rolled and tied, simplify setting the table.

**Flatware**, *far right*
Stainless and other daily-use flatware can be kept at the ready by simply displaying it in glasses or other attractive containers.

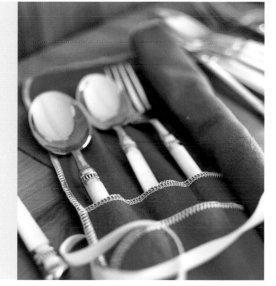

Food just seems to taste better when eaten out-of-doors. Take advantage of this fact by setting an inviting table on the deck, on a lawn under the trees, in a courtyard, or on a poolside patio. Entertaining outdoors is ideal because it lets you enjoy both the planning and the party. You can let Mother Nature do the big decorating, and focus instead on adding the special details that complement a natural setting – comfortable seating, a strikingly set table, and dramatic lighting. Whether you

# DINING
# OUTDOORS

A DINING SPACE IN THE BACKYARD, ON A MOUNTAINSIDE, OR AT WATER'S EDGE IS NATURALLY APPEALING. LET NATURE TAKE CARE OF THE DECOR, AND MAKE COMFORT YOUR PRIORITY.

have a smallish city balcony or a sprawling backyard patio, you can easily make outdoor dining a habit throughout the warm season. Start by equipping your space with furnishings that stand up to the elements. Today's options for water-resistant furniture and fabrics are nearly boundless, and you can now enjoy indoor comfort and style in outdoor areas without worries about the weather forecast. Then, to ensure a relaxed, convivial mood (and to lighten your workload), serve food buffet- or family-style, asking guests to pass dishes among themselves. When there are new faces in the crowd, there's no better way to get conversation going.

# A Lakeside Table

Few things are more relaxing than a meal taken by a lake on a sunny day. Keep it informal with casual settings and durable dishware.

Any meal shared at the water's edge is an instant invitation for guests – and the host – to relax. When it's time to set the table, keep in step with the laid-back surroundings. Dress the table simply and casually, with a bright, breezy (and washable) cotton tablecloth and napkins, and use great-looking (and practical) acrylic glassware and durable enamelware.

One of the best ways to keep an outdoor party lively is to serve food buffet-style. Bring out a console table from indoors and lay food and refreshments on it, using sturdy dishes and serving utensils. The ideal spot is close to a kitchen window, which the cook can use as a pass-through to set out a hearty meal with ease.

## WHY THIS ROOM WORKS

A rustic lakefront dock outfitted with a durable outdoor dining set provides a mellow spot for summer meals. The summer-camp style is comfortable and familiar, cueing everyone to relax and enjoy.

■ WEATHER-RESISTANT FURNISHINGS stand up to the elements and are ready for any gathering, whether dressed up for dinner or down for game playing.

■ A RED-AND-WHITE PALETTE, played out in solids, stripes, and plaids, keeps the mood light and adds punch to the natural surroundings.

■ CASUAL ACCESSORIES like printed cotton pillows and festive striped blankets add comfort to the solid, practical furniture. Kitchen towels serve as napkins.

■ A WINDOWSILL SHELF made from an old metal sign makes a convenient serving station. The cook can pass the food through the window for guests to serve themselves. This also makes cleanup more efficient.

WHY THIS ROOM WORKS

In this poolhouse dining room, a calming palette of blue and white is played out in casual style to capture the sunny mood of long summer days.

■ **AN INDOOR-OUTDOOR MIX** of dining room luxuries and outdoor accoutrements provides comfort and invigorating freshness.

■ **AN OUTDOOR FIREPLACE** extends the season for dining out-of-doors.

■ **SEA COLORS** are carried throughout the room, from the varying patterns of block-print pillows on the chairs to the laminated fabric place mats and durable acrylic tableware. The setting is quite simple but appears elegant.

■ **NAUTICAL THEMES** abound, including bookends used to hold napkins.

DINING OUTDOORS

# Dinner by the Pool

A poolhouse or patio is a natural backdrop for summer get-togethers. Set a colorful table by the water and guests will linger for hours.

If you're fortunate enough to have a swimming pool, a dining area that's set in a poolhouse or on a poolside patio is the perfect spot for a whole season of outdoor entertaining. In such an appealing setting, not a lot of fuss is required, so you can keep things relatively simple and spend more time visiting with your guests.

Start with a summery table set for enjoying the easy pleasures of a barbecue or clambake. Durable wicker furniture, now available in a wide range of colors, naturally evokes a warm-weather mood. Set wicker chairs around the table, and make them comfortable with weatherproof cushions and pillows. Create a sea-side mood by outfitting the table in sailing colors and nautical stripes. In the summer sun, blue accents used in furnishings and tableware evoke the ocean and the deep azure of the sky at dusk. If you don't have a covered porch, be sure to keep patio umbrellas on hand for protection from direct sun or summer showers.

# A Country Setting

To add a personal touch to an outdoor meal, establish a theme based on the location, and follow it through with witty details.

Once you've found the perfect spot to spend a sunny afternoon with great friends and good food, look to the setting itself for the party's style. When you adopt a theme that's in sync with the surroundings, it's easier to put together a memorable gathering. Center your table decor around one idea — a casual harvest luncheon, an elegant lawn party. Find flowers, foliage, and branches that grow nearby to create simple centerpieces. Instead of using indoor dining chairs, scout out other options. If lunch is in the park, pull a table up to benches; if it's behind a barn, set up hay bales for seating. When it comes to food and drinks, make it easy on yourself by using disposable containers that cut down on cleanup.

## WHY THIS ROOM WORKS

A country-theme dinner set on the sunny side of a barn fits seamlessly into the landscape. Everything from the seating and table coverings to the centerpieces are inspired by the locale.

■ HAY BALE BENCHES flanking the long table are a clever seating alternative; paintbrushes at each setting double as witty clothes brushes for loose straw.

■ THE BURLAP TABLECLOTH is large enough to cover the legs of a rented folding table. A narrow length of raw linen frames the centerpieces, and small kitchen towels are used as napkins.

■ THEMED DETAILS, including a wheelbarrow ice chest and camp lanterns hung from rakes, set a lighthearted mood. Wildflowers are picked in bunches and set directly in simple glass containers — no arranging necessary.

■ TAKEOUT CONTAINERS serve as easy-care dishware and simplify food service and cleanup.

BRING STYLE OUTDOORS WITH AN EASY MENU AND PORTABLE FOOD PRESENTATIONS THAT SIMPLIFY SERVING MEALS IN A FRESH-AIR SETTING.

**An antique bottle caddy**, *opposite top*, makes it a breeze to whisk dessert out to the table. Glass tumblers set in each compartment hold waffle cones, filled with fresh fruit and wrapped in striped napkins. This serving idea has a nostalgic appeal that captures the magic of childhood summers at the beach.

**Bundled sandwiches**, *opposite bottom*, are neatly wrapped with paper napkins and bound with twine. A length of matching twine is all you need to tie together utensils. This portable serving system lets guests easily help themselves and can be prepped before a party.

**Twine-tied rocks**, *left*, anchor a tablecloth in case a breeze kicks up at a waterfront table. Table anchors can be crafted from found objects such as large seashells or smooth river stones. Tie a row of stones together with a continuous length of string, as shown here, to make them more manageable.

**Enameled bowls**, *above*, corral individual lunches into a neat package, complete with utensils and a drink. The easy-to-assemble contents are held in place with a napkin, which also functions as a convenient handle, so the bowls can be toted to the backyard or picnic.

COOKING

"THE KITCHEN REALLY IS THE HEART OF MY HOME. THIS IS MY FAVORITE PLACE BECAUSE EVERYONE GATHERS HERE, AND I CAN CATCH UP WITH FAMILY AND FRIENDS AS I COOK."

ELEMENTS OF A SUCCESSFUL

# KITCHEN

The kitchen has come into its own as a living space. Kitchens have always been essential to home life, but these days we spend more time in them and use them for a wider range of activities than ever before. Besides being larger and more open to other rooms of the home, the kitchen is now looking more like the rest of the house, incorporating elements like wood flooring, cabinetry designed to resemble furniture, and decorative accessories such as art and culinary collections. At the same time, this space is becoming more customized, with appliances and conveniences that are as forward-thinking as anything available for the home.

For the following pages, we've selected a number of rooms that demonstrate the latest ideas in making a kitchen hardworking and relaxing, well-planned and full of warmth.

# How to Plan a Kitchen

In the kitchen, functional considerations that affect how the space works are more vital to your initial planning than style decisions. Begin by establishing an efficient work triangle, the key to every well-planned kitchen.

Time-tested guidelines offer useful parameters for a well-designed kitchen. Always start with the work triangle. Simply put, the work triangle is defined by the placement of the sink, stove or cooktop, and refrigerator. An efficient work triangle minimizes how far you must walk while preparing a meal. Ideally, each leg of the triangle measures between 4 and 9 feet (1.2–2.7 m) and the sum of the three sides of the triangle should be between 16 and 26 feet (4.9–7.9 m). These dimensions also accommodate the minimum amount of counter

and storage space you'll need. The sink area ideally will include 24 inches (60 cm) of undercounter space for a dishwasher, and you should allow 30–48 inches (76–120 cm) of counter surface between the sink and the stove, which is the area where you'll spend the bulk of your time while cooking.

If two cooks regularly use your kitchen simultaneously, plan a second food preparation area around another sink, usually set in a center island. Including an island or peninsula in your plan provides more workspace for two cooks and keeps the work triangle outside the family's traffic paths (see opposite page for more about islands). Because the refrigerator is used frequently by family members between meals, it's best to position it at the outside edge of the workspace, so it can be easily accessed whether you're cooking or simply snacking.

## FAMILY KITCHEN

This room (above and preceding page) features an oversize island that has an attached kitchen table incorporated into its design. The table is the family communication center as well as a place to dine together.

■ THE EFFICIENT WORK TRIANGLE is removed from traffic, thanks to a stainless steel sink in the work end of the island.

■ A LARGE FARMHOUSE-STYLE sink sits well out of the way of food preparation, so kids and other noncooks can use it easily.

■ COUNTER HEIGHTS are varied for different tasks; the tabletop is 30" (76 cm) high, the standard for dining and also a baker's dream: the ideal counter height for kneading dough is 28–32" (71–81 cm).

■ COUNTER AND STORAGE SPACE is maximized in this L-shaped configuration.

FAMILY ROOM

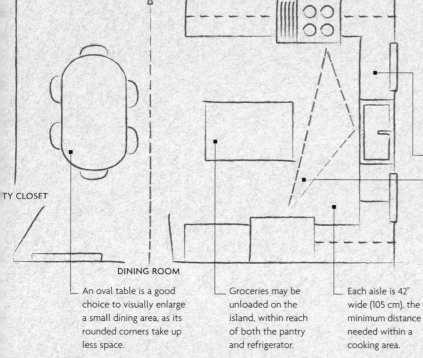

TY CLOSET

DINING ROOM

## U-SHAPED EAT-IN KITCHEN

This combination kitchen–dining area is organized in a U-shaped plan, one of the most efficient possibilities because it results in long stretches of counter surface and cabinet storage.

The main food preparation area has a generous 4' (1.2 m) length of counter space.

The work triangle is out of the way of foot traffic passing through the room.

An oval table is a good choice to visually enlarge a small dining area, as its rounded corners take up less space.

Groceries may be unloaded on the island, within reach of both the pantry and refrigerator.

Each aisle is 42" wide (105 cm), the minimum distance needed within a cooking area.

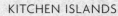

## KITCHEN ISLANDS

Islands are an efficient way to add extra storage and work surface to your kitchen. If the island includes a sink or stovetop, it can tighten the work triangle and save steps.

### Island Size
Ideal dimensions for islands call for a 3'-high (90 cm) work counter that is at least 25" (66 cm) deep. A breakfast bar side may be taller than the counter side. It should be 4' (1.2 m) high to fit stools for seating, and at least 14" (36 cm) deep.

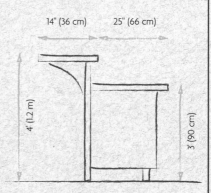

14" (36 cm)     25" (66 cm)

4' (1.2 m)                    3' (90 cm)

### Room Size
A kitchen island requires a room that's at least 8 x 12' (2.4 x 3.5 m) to accommodate it comfortably.

### Efficiency
If you have two cooks in the family, it's helpful to have two sinks, one located in the island, to help establish dual preparation areas.

### Materials
You can use materials on the island that match or complement the cabinetry, but many cooks choose ones that differ from surrounding countertops. If you enjoy baking, opt for a marble counter to keep dough cool and workable. Or go with something totally different. A free-standing farmhouse table or a stainless steel worktable used as an island can form an intriguing centerpiece.

### Customized Storage
Capitalize on storage space within an island by fitting deeper shelves that hold bowls and pots on the cooking side, and shallow shelves for glassware on the dining side. Open storage under an island is a great place for appliances and bulky cookware that won't fit in standard cabinets.

## OPEN GALLEY

The biggest drawback of a galley kitchen – the feeling of a tight enclosure – is eliminated when the kitchen is part of an open-plan space. Use common materials throughout all areas to integrate the kitchen seamlessly.

A TV cabinet in the living area is crafted in a similar style and material as the kitchen cabinetry, to help unify the open plan.

When extra chairs are needed for dining, armchairs can be brought over from this seating area.

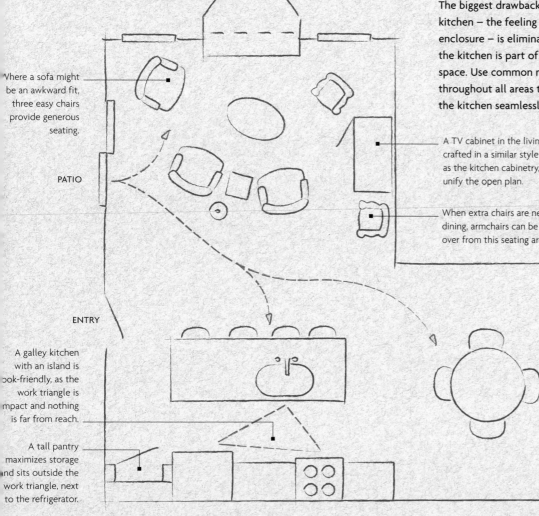

Where a sofa might be an awkward fit, three easy chairs provide generous seating.

PATIO

ENTRY

A galley kitchen with an island is cook-friendly, as the work triangle is compact and nothing is far from reach.

A tall pantry maximizes storage and sits outside the work triangle, next to the refrigerator.

Smart planning is the first step of any design, and this is especially true in the kitchen. This is a space that has to look and feel as inviting as the rest of your rooms and yet work harder than any of them. Above all, it's essential that your kitchen work *for you*. Fortunately, there are so many options for customizing a kitchen these days that everyone can benefit from new designs. Start by looking at how you'll use the space. Are you a gourmet cook, or does your busy lifestyle mean that you rely more

# DESIGNING
## YOUR DREAM KITCHEN

THE BEST KITCHENS ARE EFFICIENT HOME BASES FOR COOKING, RELAXING, AND ENTERTAINING. MAKE YOURS A JOY TO COME HOME TO AND A PLEASURE TO WORK IN.

on prepared foods? A perfect kitchen affords comfort and ease for all the things you do most often. If you and your family like to cook together, make sure you have plenty of room for separate work zones, and think about installing an extra sink. If you enjoy entertaining, perhaps an open-plan space is best, so you can be part of the fun while preparing the food. This could be the time to add a pantry, breakfast bar, or laundry closet; install dual dishwashers or a wine cabinet; or finally get that kitchen work desk you've always wanted. Dream big, then plan carefully. Kitchens demand more detailed decisions than other rooms, but the results are worth it.

# The New Classic

Built for efficiency and easy upkeep, the service kitchens of yesterday's grand estates hold valuable design lessons for today's spaces.

For a state-of-the-art kitchen, look to the past. White cabinetry, glazed subway tiles, stone countertops, and stainless steel fittings are design elements that recall the servants' kitchens of historic estates. These materials make good sense for use in today's family kitchen for the same reason they were favored then: durability. Overscale work islands, another key element in estate kitchens, allow multiple cooks to work together comfortably. A second sink installed in the island can tighten the work triangle, saving steps for the cook. Pantries, once the norm, are also making a comeback. A pantry's great advantage is that it offers efficient storage with fewer cabinets, so there's room for more windows, an asset in any kitchen.

## WHY THIS ROOM WORKS

This generously proportioned kitchen combines classic materials with up-to-date amenities and is as stylish as it is practical.

■ AN OVERSIZE ISLAND anchors the expansive space and provides an enviable work surface. Its open base offers a great deal of accessible storage on all sides but minimizes its bulk.

■ A U-SHAPED LAYOUT creates an efficient work triangle (a refrigerator, not visible, is to the right of the cooktop). A second sink, fitted in the island, diminishes the size of the triangle and puts it outside the main traffic aisle.

■ A WALK-IN PANTRY behind the cooktop wall diminishes the number of cabinets needed, freeing one wall for a bank of windows.

■ COORDINATED ACCENT MATERIALS and accessories in tin and in black and white add to the room's handsome appeal. A custom-made spice cabinet, centered within the cooktop niche, adds a simple and useful focal point.

# Smart Choices for the Home Chef

If you love to cook and want a more efficient and satisfying place to prepare meals, outfit your kitchen with features favored by the pros.

Commercial kitchens are the domain of professional chefs, but they offer ideas that you can borrow to enhance your own kitchen. Appliances with the power and efficiency of those found in restaurant kitchens are widely available in versions adapted for the home, and some modifications to kitchen materials can be made without requiring a total renovation. Choose features that suit your preferred style of cooking. For example, a marble countertop keeps pastry dough cool and firm; a faucet at the stove makes fast work of filling pots for soups or seafood boils; an island sink simplifies rinsing vegetables before chopping and cleanup afterward.

## WHY THIS ROOM WORKS

Centered around an island worktable, this kitchen for an avid cook incorporates appliances and customized storage solutions adopted from professional kitchens.

■ A RESTAURANT-STYLE STOVE is fitted with a water line and a long-necked spigot for filling pots; a rail keeps frequently used utensils organized and accessible.

■ AMPLE STORAGE is on every level, with spaces customized for specific items. Chilled wine is conveniently located in a refrigerated wine cabinet; a customized drawer keeps jars of spices organized.

■ SMALL APPLIANCES such as the mixer and toaster are home-sized versions of professional models. They deliver the power and ease of their commercial counterparts.

■ A BUILT-IN OFFICE NOOK offers a countertop for recipe planning. Shelves above hold cookbooks, food magazines, and other kitchen items.

WHY THIS ROOM WORKS

This pared-down kitchen feels more spacious than its actual square footage, thanks to its open styling. A peninsula serves as a food prep area, sideboard, and gathering spot.

■ SIMPLE MATERIALS and fixtures blend with well-edited collections to create a casual look.

■ A LARGE WINDOW floods the room with natural light, which bounces off the bright surfaces and gleaming stainless steel. Butcher-block counters lend the sunny space warmth.

■ VINTAGE GLASS CANISTERS and jars of different shapes and sizes allow the cook to easily see what's inside and also make a pleasing decorative grouping.

■ PERSONAL COLLECTIONS lining the shelves give the room character.

DESIGNING YOUR DREAM KITCHEN

# Easy Entertaining

If you're a cook who tends toward simple meals and carryout, you're free to enjoy the pleasures of a pared-down, open-style space.

For the occasional cook, an open kitchen tucked into a small space can be just what's wanted for informal entertaining and dining. Even a small kitchen can be a relaxing place to cook and congregate when the essentials are all right at hand. Keep frequently used ingredients and utensils at the cook's fingertips, and incorporate a peninsula or island into the design to allow the host and guests to carry on a conversation while preparing the food. A butcher-block–topped open counter is versatile, too. It's roomy enough to chop on and beautiful enough to serve hors d'oeuvres from at a cocktail party. It also makes a perfect sideboard for spreading out food to serve buffet-style.

Open shelves may replace overhead cabinets, leaving collections and dishware on view and expanding the room's sense of space. Using a monochromatic palette and straightforward materials like stainless steel and butcher block keeps a kitchen feeling uncluttered.

Making the most of space is a different challenge in every room. It may mean enjoying a wealth of space and customizing it for maximum comfort. It also might mean making creative use of every possible inch to provide adequate work space and increase storage potential. Whatever size room you have, it requires good space planning. In a kitchen, this means addressing two major concerns. First, there's a need to create well-designed work zones (for prep, cooking, cleanup, and

# MAXIMIZING
## YOUR KITCHEN SPACE

FROM THE LARGEST ROOM TO THE SMALLEST CABINET, ANY SPACE BENEFITS FROM A SMART SYSTEM. THE KEY TO A WELL-RUN KITCHEN IS THOUGHTFUL SPACE PLANNING.

storage) and an efficient work triangle (the setup of the refrigerator, range, and sink in relation to one another). A well-thought-out floor plan provides all of this so that your kitchen will run smoothly. The other essential in any kitchen is abundant storage. This is best achieved with a combination of inventive storage aids: variable-height shelving and compartmentalized drawers, corner lazy Susans, cookie sheet and tray racks, roll-out shelves and baskets — the options are almost endless. All these features can be added to existing cabinetry, too, so you don't need to plan a whole-room remodel to take advantage of their efficiencies.

WHY THIS ROOM WORKS

Functioning as both kitchen and dining room, this generous space is a favorite place to gather and linger for simple snacks or large dinners.

■ THE KITCHEN WORK AREA is laid out with a small work triangle for optimal ease and efficiency.

■ THE CENTER ISLAND has a dining bar built into one side, offering a spot for snacks or light meals or for guests to gather while meals are prepared.

■ AN ANTIQUE CUPBOARD in the dining area keeps china and linens close at hand, and brings the warmth and personality often associated with other rooms into the kitchen space.

■ BUTLER'S PANTRY–STYLE CABINETS and beadboard trim give an appealing vintage look to the open space.

MAXIMIZING YOUR KITCHEN SPACE

# The Eat-In Kitchen

Bring together the pleasures of cooking, eating, and entertaining with a hardworking kitchen that incorporates a roomy, graceful dining area.

Real estate listings herald an "eat-in kitchen" for good reason. Many families covet a kitchen–dining room setup that can be used for gatherings great and small. Such a plan retains the warmth that is among an eat-in kitchen's best assets but adds an uncommon sense of spaciousness. By combining a kitchen and dining room, you can bring a greater feeling of flow to your home's layout. It also allows you to allocate different areas to different kinds of dining. Weekday breakfasts, informal lunches, and quick meals can be served at a dining bar designed as part of a kitchen island; family suppers and dinner parties may be enjoyed at a large table in the dedicated dining area. A center island is ideal for entertaining, as it allows guests to gather during meal preparation and lets the cook feel like part of the party even while working. For the most harmonious effect, the kitchen and dining decor should complement each other but be subtly different, as befits their purposes.

# A Ship-Shape Galley

Give a narrow kitchen all the advantages of a larger one. Smart planning makes a galley kitchen a room that's a pleasure to work in.

A galley kitchen – which takes its name from ships' galleys, where space is notoriously tight – is one of the realities of many urban homes and apartments. Though a galley kitchen may not be terribly spacious, it can be wonderfully efficient. One of its greatest assets is the compact size of its work triangle, which ensures that nothing is ever far from the cook's reach and makes the room an enjoyable workspace. One common disadvantage is a lack of space for storage, but this can be remedied. Specialized cabinetry like shallow pantry-style cabinets, pull-out pantry towers, and custom-built drawers make use of every inch; special appliances in smaller-than-normal sizes take up less space.

## WHY THIS ROOM WORKS

This galley kitchen is quite narrow, but it gives the illusion of being larger due to its all-white color palette. Materials and textures are limited to just a few, and the counters are kept uncluttered, further enhancing an open feel.

■ AN OPTIMAL WORK TRIANGLE is achieved in the small room: stove, sink, and refrigerator (on the wall opposite the stove) are all within easy reach of a cook.

■ SHALLOW WALL CABINETS are not the standard 12–15" (30–38 cm) deep, but instead are pantry-style, just deep enough for one row of items. Because of their shallow depth, they're able to be flush-mounted to avoid any overhang of the counter below.

■ A WALL-MOUNTED FAUCET saves precious inches, further enhancing the streamlined look of the room.

■ HIDDEN DRAWERS behind white cabinet doors preserve the room's clean-lined effect.

# Creative Storage

The best ways to use space aren't always merely functional. Be clever about using the space you have and bring style to storage.

One of the most crucial elements of space planning in the kitchen is storage. Nearly everyone wishes they had more of it, customized to fit every cooking item. With a little ingenuity, you can create more room for storage and give your kitchen a personalized look at the same time. Begin by customizing every space you can. Subdivide storage compartments with decorative trays, baskets, bowls, and racks. Put items that you use every day like napkins and silverware into a basket and leave it in a spot convenient to the dining table. Where there's room, make decorative displays of produce or other common necessities. Corral cooking oils and vinegars in a rimmed tray and leave it out on the countertop.

## WHY THIS ROOM WORKS

This spacious kitchen with its generous center island features a combination of fixed and moveable storage containers, offering a multitude of flexible options.

■ OPEN AND CLOSED STORAGE compartments are designed into the island, allowing easy access to frequently used essentials but concealing lesser used items.

■ BASKETS WITH CUTOUT HANDLES form an orderly grid that conceals towels, snacks, and spices.

■ FLEA-MARKET TREASURES are repurposed for storage: a bottle drying rack is pressed into service as a cup holder.

■ DECORATIVE TRAYS keep hard-to-organize items like flatware and condiments neat and portable.

■ THE CASUAL DECOR of warm wood cabinets, salvaged wood beams, and a rustic metal vent hood are a handsome backdrop for the unique collectibles on display.

# Cabinetry Options

Your choice of cabinetry defines your kitchen's style, so it's often the first consideration after establishing a space plan. Whether you prefer open or closed cabinets or a mix of both, the range of choices is tremendous, with each style offering different material, frame, and finish options. Face-frame cabinets, whose doors have a raised frame around the center panel, are more classic; frameless cabinets are completely flat-fronted and afford a more streamlined look. Stock cabinets save money, though they offer fewer choices in style. With so many organizing systems now available, stock cabinets can be easily fittted with custom storage accessories. Semi-custom cabinets offer more diverse finishes as well as superior materials and construction. Fully custom cabinets offer high-end details like self-closing drawers, pull-out pantries, spice or knife drawers, and toe-kick drawers – the options are almost endless. For more information, see Materials, page 360.

**Wooden lower cabinets**, *right*, are paired with stainless-steel shelves to make efficient and attractive use of this wall. A mix of open and closed storage options is a smart way to put attractive items on view while keeping more utilitarian pieces behind closed doors.

## DESIGN LESSON **PANTRY STORAGE**

It used to be that pantries were separate rooms off the kitchen, designed for containing all the ingredients that a cook needed. These days, the definition of a pantry has expanded to include built-in towers or freestanding cabinets, often customized with an array of special storage fittings. Within a tall storage unit, shelves roll out or are only the depth of one can or box, so all your stored supplies are visible at a glance. Not only can you spot things quickly, there's no need to move things out from the front to get to items near the back. Pantries don't have to be large to be efficient, and they can be carved out of overlooked spaces, too, such as underneath a stairway, along the walls of the basement stairs, or in an underused kitchen corner.

■ **TAKE ADVANTAGE OF FITTINGS** like door ladders, swing-out or roll-out baskets and shelves, and lazy Susans, to make maximum use of pantry space. The ability to pull items out toward you is essential in deep cabinets or closets, where items in the back are difficult to access.

■ **DOOR-MOUNTED SHELVES** add efficiency to a pantry space. All shelving fitted here should have a lip or restraint on the front to prevent items from falling off when the door is opened or closed.

■ **CREATE SEPARATE ZONES** for different items – canned goods, baking ingredients, packaged foods, etc. – to make it easier to find what you need and stay organized.

**Glass-Front Doors**, *right*
Doors with glass panes appeal for different reasons. Some people like the look of turn-of-the-century butler's pantry cabinets, which commonly had multiple panes of glass; some cooks just like to see their well-filled larders. Glass doors also help a small kitchen appear larger.

**Translucent Doors**, *far right*
Translucent panes on cabinets are a distinctive way to let light into a kitchen. Here, frosted glass doors are mounted in front of a window, maximizing both light and storage. Bowls and vases are silhouetted by the outside light in a unique abstract presentation.

**Wood**, *right*
Wood remains the top choice for kitchen cabinets. Wood not only is durable, but also can be easily stained, painted, or glazed to suit any decor. Frames, panels, and moulding add character for a traditional look; frameless wood can be quite contemporary.

**Laminate**, *far right*
Laminated cabinets have an up-to-date appeal that can be striking when paired with warm wood flooring or furniture. Laminates require less care than wood and are stain- and scuff-resistant. Vinyl and laminate cabinets are available in even more varieties than wood, in matte, textured, and gloss finishes.

### Roll-Out Shelves

Fitting low cabinets or a pantry with roll-out shelves saves you having to bend or squat to remove things. Sliding trays similar to this one can be retrofitted into existing cabinets for a modest cost. Their drawer-like construction prevents objects from sliding off when the shelf is being rolled in or out.

### Deep Drawers

A deep drawer keeps things more accessible than a deep shelf does because items located at the back can be found and taken out more easily. Drawer storage of bottles works best when the drawer is divided into sections and each section is fairly full. This helps prevent bottles from shifting and toppling.

### Under-Appliance Drawer

A shallow drawer built under an appliance or cabinet is a great example of efficient use of space. This one, tucked under a stove, is perfectly situated for corralling baking sheets and assorted tins and molds. Toe-kick drawers can be installed to capitalize on space under almost any cabinet, and there are even folding stepladders that fit in a toe-kick space.

### Pegboard Dividers

A pegboard system provides flexible options for organizing drawers. Push pegs into the holes to separate and steady items. This adjustable storage solution works for virtually any kind of object — stacks of dishes and teacups, spice jars, linens, cooking implements — whatever you may need to organize in your drawers.

### Island Storage

Make the most of space within a kitchen island by incorporating both deep and shallow storage into it. On the cooking side, 24"- deep (60 cm) cabinets hide large cooking equipment. On the dining side, shallow shelves utilize space that might otherwise be wasted. A colorful display of tableware brightens and personalizes this island.

### Adjustable Shelves

Installing adjustable shelves or slide-out drawers inside cabinets is a simple and inexpensive way to tailor storage to your specific needs and accommodate assorted sizes of cookware. Allow 1–3" (3–8 cm) of space between the tallest item and the next shelf, to facilitate moving items in and out.

# Under-Counter Storage Options

The areas under your counters are usually the largest storage spaces in your kitchen. To maximize space and keep it organized, customize the shelves, drawers, or racks to suit your needs. There are many ready-made fittings now available that you can install in existing cabinetry to replace or add to fixed shelves. Fit rollout shelves into deep cupboards to make it simpler to find what you need; add dividers to deep drawers, sectioning them into quadrants; attach racks to the insides of cabinet doors. Use adjustable shelving, and set the shelves at heights customized for specific contents. Group like items by size and by task, then keep groups nearest their work zone – pots near the stove, oils near the prep area, towels and sponges next to the clean-up zone, and so on. Assign a spot to each and every item in the kitchen, and you'll never wonder where anything has gone.

**Open shelves beneath the stove**, *left*, are the perfect spot for pots and pans, providing quick access to them for the cook. Heavy-duty shelving can also hold small appliances, freeing up counter space.

---

## DESIGN LESSON **ADJUST THE HEIGHT TO FIT**

While specialized built-in storage is one of the benefits of custom cabinetry, another increasingly popular advantage is the ability to adjust the height of the working counter to fit the cook. All standard base cabinets are 36" (90 cm) high, a comfortable working height for the general population. Taller cooks can install cabinets that bring the work surface up to as high as 45" (114 cm), eliminating straining and awkward bending at the counter. Cooks come in all sizes, and recent research into repetitive-stress injuries and ergonomics indicates that the best work surfaces vary in height depending on the task. Besides adjusting counter height, you may also want to modify shelf and wall-oven installations for maximum comfort.

■ COUNTER HEIGHT: Chopping, kneading dough, and mixing by hand are more comfortable on a surface that is 28–32" (70–80 cm) high. Many cooks instinctively move to a table, whose height allows them to fully extend their arms while working.

■ OVEN PLACEMENT: The bottom of a wall oven should not be higher than waist level, to avoid burning your arms on the open door as you remove a heated dish.

■ STORAGE HEIGHT: Shelves and cabinets between your knee and eye level are the ones you can most comfortably reach without stretching. It's not practical to limit storage to that area, but use this guideline for storing things you use often.

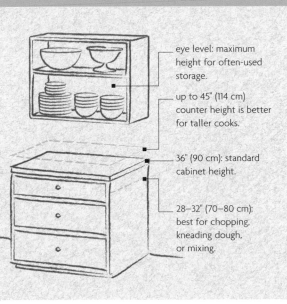

eye level: maximum height for often-used storage.

up to 45" (114 cm) counter height is better for taller cooks.

36" (90 cm): standard cabinet height.

28–32" (70–80 cm): best for chopping, kneading dough, or mixing.

For most people, the kitchen is the hub around which the whole family revolves. So it makes sense that the decor of a kitchen should reflect the tastes and interests of the family it serves. There's no denying that care for decorative items is a concern here, since cooking and cleaning can be damaging to delicate pieces. Turn this fact to your advantage and tell your style story in ways that are uniquely appropriate to this space. This means decorating with items that are beautifully durable. The

# EXPRESSING
## YOUR STYLE

THE KITCHEN IS ONE OF A HOME'S MOST ESSENTIAL SPACES. ENHANCE YOURS WITH COLLECTIONS AND TREASURES THAT SPEAK VOLUMES ABOUT YOU AND YOUR FAMILY.

most obvious first choice is culinary-related pieces. Everyday items like cookbooks, crockery, servingware, and flavored vinegars are naturals for kitchen displays. Collectibles like vintage linens, salt and pepper shakers, cookie jars and canisters, or antique kitchen tools also have great visual appeal. If you have a number of collections, you can rearrange or swap them for a quick change of style in the room. Plants and botanicals are another smart option. Herbs can be grown in pots or boxes, trimmed as topiaries, or dried and hung. And children's artwork is always a favorite choice, bringing warmth and whimsy to this family-oriented space.

WHY THIS ROOM WORKS

This open-plan dining room and kitchen has an appealing flow to its space, good definition of zones, and a cohesive sense of style.

■ THE ISLAND COUNTER is higher on the dining side and lower on the food preparation side, so it conceals working countertops from diners.

■ AN OPEN HANGING PLATE RACK above the island completes the see-through "wall" separating the two areas.

■ CONSISTENT COLORS AND MATERIALS are used throughout the space, and a red accent color is seen repeatedly throughout the three zones.

■ A NATURAL WOVEN RUG defines the dining and lounging areas.

■ LARGE-SCALE WINDOWS expand the space and flood all areas with sunlight.

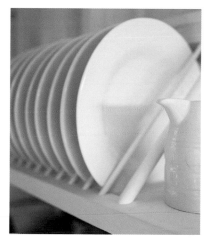

EXPRESSING YOUR STYLE

# An Open Approach

Create a sense of harmony in an open-plan room by maintaining a continuity of style that reflects the beauty of the rest of your home.

You have no doubt seen and read a lot about open-plan spaces, or "great rooms." These multipurpose rooms offer countless possibilities for configuring the ways you cook, dine, and entertain. The first step in making an open-plan kitchen and dining area work is to look at the space as a whole rather than approaching it as two different rooms. Strive to bring to it the overall style of your home. Give it a cohesive look by using the same flooring and other materials in both areas, and paint the walls the same color – or carry an accent color from one area to the next. Subtly suggest division between the spaces in ways that maintain a sense of openness. Use beams or other architectural markers, hanging pot- or plate racks, furniture placement, or area rugs to indicate zones. This is especially important if your plan includes a living room. The more space you have, the more it needs to be shaped to create functional areas that are distinct yet display your style.

# Simply White

An all-white kitchen is a fresh and bright decorating choice that delivers dramatic impact with understated, elegant style.

Sometimes the best way to make a strong statement is with silence. The same is true in decorating. An absence of color can make as strong a personal declaration as a showy abundance of it. An all-white color scheme also has the benefit of feeling fresh, clean, and bright, qualities that are especially desirable in a kitchen. The best complement for an all-white room is a wealth of natural light, which enlivens any space. Leave windows uncovered, or partially covered with sheers or bottom-mount shades, to maximize sunlight streaming in. Mix shades of white in matte and gloss surfaces with clear glass pieces, and combine various shapes, textures, and patterns to give the room warmth and dynamism.

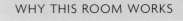

## WHY THIS ROOM WORKS

A pure white color scheme, carried out in everything from the furnishings to the trim and tableware, makes this kitchen feel fresh and especially soothing.

■ HIGH-GLOSS PAINT transforms a simple wooden dining set into a striking furnishing choice.

■ SUBSTANTIAL SHELVES and brackets provide welcome architectural detail on an otherwise plain wall.

■ MATERIALS AND FIXTURES are practical and modest, yet convey a sense of elegance due to the calm harmony of hues.

■ OPEN STORAGE suits the simple and casual aesthetic of the room.

■ A TABLEWARE COLLECTION of mixed contemporary and antique pieces adds texture and interest to the room. The cool and warm tones of the white and transparent pieces give the arrangement movement and visual variety.

BRING PERSONAL TOUCHES INTO
YOUR KITCHEN WITH ART, FAMILY
PHOTOS, AND COLLECTIONS THAT
ADD WHIMSY AND CHARACTER.

**Antique graters**, *opposite top*, hang in
the empty space on the side of a cabinet.
Unique collections often spark conversation in the kitchen. Every favorite object
holds a story about its origin, whether a
memorable family trip or just a day
wandering a flea market.

**A corkboard**, *opposite bottom*, fitted with
colorful thumbtacks, makes a decorative
statement. Covered with family photos,
mementos, invitations, and postcards, it
becomes an ever-changing scrapbook open
to everyone who enters the kitchen.

**A favorite painting**, *left*, warms the sleek
surfaces of a kitchen. With the simple
addition of two pears to the scale, a
pleasing still-life is formed. Keep delicate
artwork in a kitchen away from the sink
and range, because moisture and grease
may damage artwork.

**A magnetic board**, *above*, offers a
handsome alternative to covering
a refrigerator with magnets. Here, it's
mounted on a wall between cabinets
and counter, and holds recipes for the
week's menu planning.

# SLEEPING

"MY BEDROOM IS A PRIVATE SPACE DESIGNED FOR PURE COMFORT. I NEED IT TO BE FILLED WITH INVITING MATERIALS, SOFT TEXTURES, AND FAVORITE MEMENTOS."

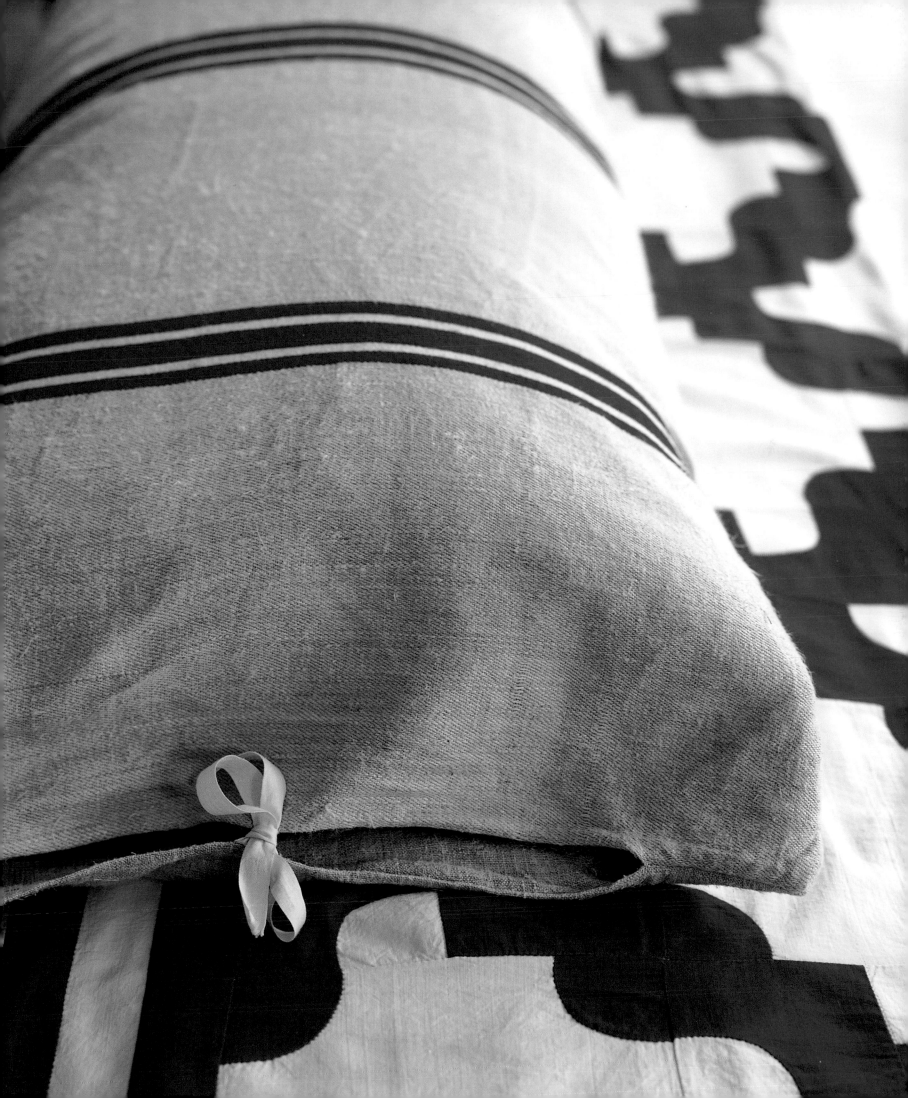

ELEMENTS OF A SUCCESSFUL

# BEDROOM

The more time we spend at home, the more important comfort and flexibility become in our rooms. In the bedroom, where we may not only sleep but also exercise, work, unwind with family, and watch television, this is more true than ever. Bedrooms today need to accommodate all these functions while preserving a sense of peace and privacy.

As bedrooms become more multifunctional, they also become more open to inspired arrangements and styling that's in keeping with the home's other spaces. A sleeping space can go beyond the traditional setup of bed, dresser, and two nightstands arranged in a standard configuration. The rooms we show you in these pages offer some new ways to start thinking about your bedroom, to help you create a space that meets your needs for both function and comfort.

# How to Plan a Bedroom

To some people, the bedroom is exclusively for resting. Others view it as a multiuse space. No matter how you see the room, the fact remains: we spend a third of our lives in bed. Invest in the best quality and comfort.

The placement of the bed is the first consideration in planning bedroom layout. Ideally a bed should be positioned with the headboard against the wall and 24 inches (60 cm) of space on either side for access and ease of making the bed (12 inches/30 cm can suffice in a pinch). In terms of style, see pages 180–81 for information about selecting a bed that best suits you.

Storage is the next concern. Organized storage in the bedroom remains high on the wish list for most people and can be achieved by using closets efficiently (see opposite page) and with dressers, wardrobes, armoires, chiffoniers, or under-bed storage. Most standard dressers have a depth of 20–22 inches (51–56 cm); allow 42–48 inches (107–120 cm) of clear space in front to open doors and drawers (30 inches/76 cm is the minimum in very tight spaces). Clothes cabinets like wardrobes and armoires tend to have a greater variance in depth and require the same clearance in front.

Bedside tables are another necessity. There should be enough room for books and magazines, a lamp both for ambient lighting and to shed light on reading, and an alarm clock, a carafe, or other amenities that you like to keep at hand. Furnishings intended for other rooms are also welcome in the bedroom: bring in a glass-front china cabinet to showcase collections, for instance, or a console table with shelves to hold reading materials.

## A LIVE-WORK BEDROOM

This soothing space is a comfortable haven by day or night. Its thoughtful design allows a workspace to be incorporated while keeping the focus on the room's main function: relaxation.

■ **A HANDSOME WORKSTATION** set in front of a bank of windows lets the bed take center stage and creates a separate work zone that feels separate and unobtrusive.

■ **RECESSED BOOKSHELVES** are streamlined and attractive, and make plenty of room for office books as well as for personal reading materials and favorite objects.

■ **MULTIPLE LIGHTING SOURCES** provide ample light for all tasks. Layered draperies allow sunshine to be let in and controlled during the day and can block out light completely in the evenings.

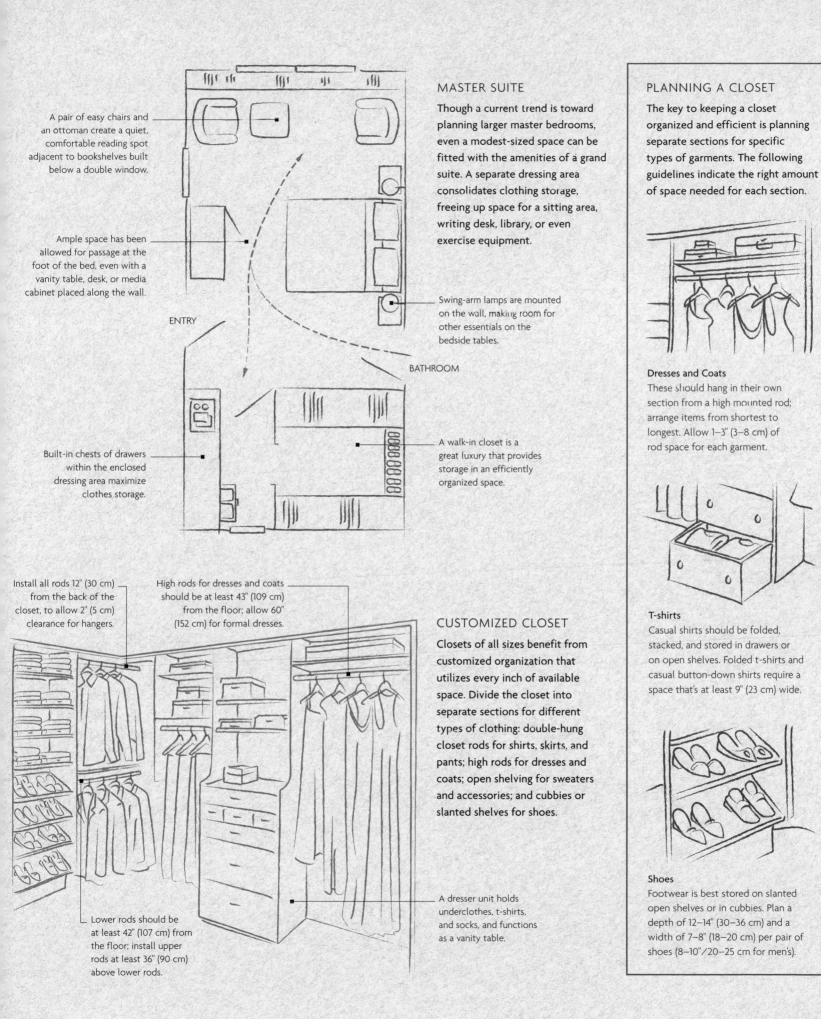

A pair of easy chairs and an ottoman create a quiet, comfortable reading spot adjacent to bookshelves built below a double window.

Ample space has been allowed for passage at the foot of the bed, even with a vanity table, desk, or media cabinet placed along the wall.

ENTRY

Built-in chests of drawers within the enclosed dressing area maximize clothes storage.

BATHROOM

Swing-arm lamps are mounted on the wall, making room for other essentials on the bedside tables.

A walk-in closet is a great luxury that provides storage in an efficiently organized space.

## MASTER SUITE

Though a current trend is toward planning larger master bedrooms, even a modest-sized space can be fitted with the amenities of a grand suite. A separate dressing area consolidates clothing storage, freeing up space for a sitting area, writing desk, library, or even exercise equipment.

## PLANNING A CLOSET

The key to keeping a closet organized and efficient is planning separate sections for specific types of garments. The following guidelines indicate the right amount of space needed for each section.

**Dresses and Coats**
These should hang in their own section from a high mounted rod; arrange items from shortest to longest. Allow 1–3" (3–8 cm) of rod space for each garment.

**T-shirts**
Casual shirts should be folded, stacked, and stored in drawers or on open shelves. Folded t-shirts and casual button-down shirts require a space that's at least 9" (23 cm) wide.

**Shoes**
Footwear is best stored on slanted open shelves or in cubbies. Plan a depth of 12–14" (30–36 cm) and a width of 7–8" (18–20 cm) per pair of shoes (8–10"/20–25 cm for men's).

Install all rods 12" (30 cm) from the back of the closet, to allow 2" (5 cm) clearance for hangers.

High rods for dresses and coats should be at least 43" (109 cm) from the floor; allow 60" (152 cm) for formal dresses.

## CUSTOMIZED CLOSET

Closets of all sizes benefit from customized organization that utilizes every inch of available space. Divide the closet into separate sections for different types of clothing: double-hung closet rods for shirts, skirts, and pants; high rods for dresses and coats; open shelving for sweaters and accessories; and cubbies or slanted shelves for shoes.

Lower rods should be at least 42" (107 cm) from the floor; install upper rods at least 36" (90 cm) above lower rods.

A dresser unit holds underclothes, t-shirts, and socks, and functions as a vanity table.

A bedroom is much more than a place to sleep. It's a retreat, a place in which to leave behind the stresses of the day and regain serenity. To make your bedroom a haven that you look forward to returning to every evening, furnish it exclusively with the textures and colors that calm you. Perhaps you've experienced the sense of having found a perfect retreat at a spa or luxury hotel. Recall that space and its relaxing effects. Remember the sumptuous fabrics and bed coverings,

# CREATING A
# SANCTUARY

THE BEDROOM IS THE MOST PERSONAL ROOM IN THE HOME. LOOK FOR WAYS TO MAKE IT A PLACE THAT YOU LONG TO RETURN TO AT THE END OF THE DAY.

the fresh fragrances in the room, the calming color palette, and the sunlight playing across the furnishings. These are all elements you can bring into your own home. Find bedding fabrics, throws, and soft pillows that you love to nestle into, and layer the bed with them. Bring bouquets of flowers into the room to add soothing scent. Choose window coverings that let in sunshine during the daytime, and light a fire or clusters of candles to add a warming glow at night. Surround yourself with family photos and favorite treasures. The right combination of simple elements transforms an ordinary bedroom into a personal sanctuary.

# A Natural Light

To create a naturally refreshing space, take advantage of an abundance of windows and embrace sunlight's soothing warmth.

Often, the first impulse for window treatments in a bedroom is heavy draperies. But natural light is so elementally restorative and soothing that we may do better inviting it in than shutting it out. Waking to wisps of daylight filtering through a window is a much calmer way to start a day than being jarred by a radio or alarm.

Covering windows in sheer draperies provides daytime privacy (hang shades or a double rod to layer on opaque coverings for nighttime) and allows in plenty of glare-free light. Choose a white or monochromatic palette and use a light touch with accents, and you'll have a naturally calm, refreshing room. Introduce lots of comforting textures for tactile pleasure and visual interest.

## WHY THIS ROOM WORKS

Oversize windows and a creamy-white palette make this bedroom a haven that revels in natural daylight. The unifying use of white, carried out through a sophisticated mix of layered textures, projects serenity.

■ SHEER WINDOW COVERINGS on the large windows diffuse daylight, provide some daytime privacy, and add romance to the atmosphere.

■ RICH TEXTURES are everywhere: hemstitch, matelassé, and faux-fur bedding, an abundance of pillows and throws, and a textured wool rug.

■ A GENEROUS MIRROR placed opposite the window reflects daylight throughout the room.

■ A RAISED HEARTH gives the fireplace more focus and makes it visible even when lying in bed.

■ EASY CHAIRS, an ottoman, and a side table make the fireside an inviting spot for reading.

## WHY THIS ROOM WORKS

Clean surfaces and a calming natural color palette give this bedroom the feel of a meditative retreat. Plush yet simple furnishings add a welcome layer of luxury.

■ NEUTRAL TONES in the bedding, upholstered furniture, and woven rug and baskets extend a restful palette that begins with calming green walls.

■ LINEN PANELS are hung over bookshelves to give them a streamlined look and minimize visual clutter.

■ ROWS OF BASKETS tucked into the bed platform contain and conceal clothing and necessities.

■ GENEROUS CHAISE LONGUES face toward the window views, creating an area for quiet relaxation.

CREATING A SANCTUARY

# Room for Reflection

A subdued palette and clever storage work together to eliminate distractions, making this bedroom a space for quiet contemplation.

Muted tones of colors found in nature are ideal for a bedroom: the browns and grays of tree bark and weathered wood, the rich creams of sand and stone, the fresh greens of spring and summer, and the cool blues of water and sky. Quiet natural colors, paired with uncluttered surfaces and smooth, cool-to-the-touch fabrics, create a contemplative, restful space.

Bring in furniture and accessories that extend the muted palette and are soft by design – chaise longues, chenille throws, an upholstered headboard, or an upholstered cube used as a nightstand. Reinforce the calming effect by minimizing visual clutter; you can even drape shelves with linen panels to conceal their contents. Find storage systems that are both visually appealing and useful. Baskets fit in all kinds of nooks and crannies, and they add pleasing texture. If you have a fireplace or a view, orient the furniture toward it to take advantage of a natural focal point for meditation.

# Colorfully Calm

Borrow aspects of Eastern interiors to transform your bedroom into a colorful yet peaceful space for rest and reflection.

The art of repose is one that has been perfected by Eastern cultures. Integrating Asian design elements into your space – bamboo, silks, tapestries, and rugs – can conjure a sense of calm even in a vividly colored room. Though subdued colors are most often thought of as calming, bright colors can also be used to evoke a restful atmosphere that's accented with exotic flair.

The use of screens, both as dividers and as decorative elements, is also an Asian tradition that translates well to a bedroom sanctuary. To subtly divide spaces in your room while adding a sense of romance, use carved or papered screens, or hang sheer panels of fabric from the ceiling to define areas and diffuse light.

## WHY THIS ROOM WORKS

Vibrant colors and see-through fabric scrims create a restful atmosphere that evokes the romance of a Far East journey.

■ VOILE PANELS hung from the ceiling delicately describe a "pavilion" around the bed. Attached with Velcro to bookcases, they also soften the strong lines and create a sense of unity throughout the room.

■ A PLATFORM-STYLE BED reinforces the Asian theme and preserves a sense of openness in the space.

■ CRISP WHITE SHEETS, a pale pink duvet, and silk shibori pillows cool down the hot colors.

■ INTRICATE MOTIFS and well-chosen accents – kilim rugs, embroidered linens, and an Asian-inspired teapot – lend an exotic touch.

■ OVERSCALE GLASS DOORS open the room up to the backyard. The scrim fabric's translucence ensures that light and views are not obscured.

# Bed Options

Today's beds are more luxurious and comfortable than ever, with an ever-widening range of sizes, materials, and styles to choose from. Given the amount of time that we spend in bed, choosing the right one is among the most significant furnishing decisions you'll make when decorating a bedroom.

Keep in mind that a bed's frame is larger than the mattress it holds, so take this into account when you're selecting a bed. Choose a frame with a sturdy headboard that offers solid support for reading. If you have lots of room, choose a frame that also has a footboard, for a finished look. If space is tight, opt for a frame with a slim headboard and no footboard. Platform beds forgo both head- and footboards, providing a completely pared-down look. Whatever style you choose, allow adequate space around the sides and end for traffic flow. A clearance of 24–36 inches (60–90 cm) lets you maneuver most comfortably.

A **platform bed**, *right*, is a wonderfully versatile style, since it has no head- or footboard and can be positioned anywhere in a room. Here it's pushed against the wall and piled with pillows, giving it the look of an attractive daybed that invites reading or lounging.

## DESIGN LESSON CARING FOR BED LINENS

From a basic set of sheets to decorative shams and duvet covers, bed linens provide a relatively inexpensive and easy way to refresh a bedroom. Good-quality cotton sheets start at 200 threads per inch; the higher the thread count, the finer the quality of the sheet. The softness and luster of cotton sheets are generally enhanced with each laundering. You can lengthen the life of your bed linens by paying attention to the way they're cleaned and stored.

To store sheets, blankets, and pillows, choose a space with good air circulation. Keep fibers fresh and dry by placing linens in unlined closets or drawers, unstained open-weave baskets, or acid-free cardboard boxes with loose-fitting lids.

■ WASH SHEETS ALONE, not with towels or other rough materials that can weaken the fabric's fibers.

■ USE COOL WATER and the gentle cycle on the washing machine to keep sheeting fibers strong. Select the extra rinse cycle if available; soap residue decreases the softness of linens.

■ SELECT COOL DRYER SETTINGS because heat weakens cotton fibers. Remove linens while slightly damp if you're going to iron them. Iron embroidered or lace pieces on the reverse side.

■ DRY-CLEAN COTTON BLANKETS that have a loose weave; washing them distorts the pattern.

■ PROTECT PILLOWS by encasing them in washable zippered protectors. Follow the care label for washing instructions, and use a low dryer setting to dry. Store unused pillows in a dry place.

## Sleigh Bed

The graceful curves of the traditional wooden sleigh-style bed have endured over time. Today, sleigh beds are also available in iron, and some models have modified, open footboards. If you choose a classic wooden frame, head- and footboards are available in differing heights and styles.

## Leather

Leather evokes the luxurious appeal of a cushiony club chair. In the bedroom, leather makes a bold statement that adds depth to the decor and brings immediate attention to the bed as a focal point. Tufted leather headboards, like the one shown here, create the ultimate comfort for reading in bed.

## Iron and Brass Beds

Antique and reproduction iron or brass beds are an enduringly popular choice. An antique frame will require a new mattress that's up to date in comfort, and some may require a custom-size mattress to fit their smaller frames. New reproductions look every bit as appealing as originals, and are more readily available.

## Wooden Panel

If you have limited space but still want the finished look and stability of a headboard, choose one with a very slim profile. You can also make one from a panel of wood, attached either to the wall or the bed frame. Paint, stencil, or stain the wood any color that coordinates with your space.

## Natural Fiber

Wicker, cane, seagrass, and other natural fibers are striking choices for headboards. The simple silhouettes of natural-fiber bed frames bring casual, warm-weather style to a bedroom, and their textured open weaves have a lighter, airier effect than solid headboards.

## Slipcovered

Swathing a headboard in fabric softens a bed and makes a more comfortable backrest for reading. Your choices are legion — go with stripes or solid linen for a tailored look, or floral cottons for romance. Slipcovered styles can camouflage existing headboards and can be removed for cleaning or refreshed with each season.

In the bedroom, where most of our personal belongings are stored, space is always a precious commodity. One of the most obvious ways to make the best use of space here is to eliminate clutter by keeping drawers and closets well organized. But there are many other ways to make a room more efficient. Take advantage of unused wall space and recessed nooks, especially under sloped or low ceilings where freestanding furniture may not fit. Tuck an inviting window seat, with storage built

# MAKING THE MOST OF
# YOUR SPACE

WHETHER YOU HAVE A WEALTH OF SPACE FOR A BEDROOM OR VERY LITTLE, MAKE THE MOST OF IT. CREATIVE PLANNING HELPS A ROOM ACHIEVE ITS GREATEST POTENTIAL.

into its base, into a sun-filled dormer. Fit other niches with customized shelving or built-in bureau drawers. Using every recess available in a space increases a room's functionality – and its character. Armoires and other storage cabinets come in many sizes and styles and are hardworking and handsome additions to a bedroom. Choosing well-proportioned and appropriately scaled pieces also visually expands a space. In a small bedroom, furniture that is slim and scaled-down or high off the floor adds to an impression of greater space. In a bigger room, you have more of an opportunity to make a statement with large-scaled pieces.

WHY THIS ROOM WORKS

Crisp fabrics and fresh accents bring new life to a master bedroom suite in a former attic. Positioning the bed in the dormer provides headroom and space for side tables.

■ **A TRIANGULAR WINDOW** creatively fitted into the side of the dormer makes the room seem more spacious and allows daylight to come flooding in.

■ **SLIM FRENCH DOORS** opening out onto a small balcony are custom-fitted to the peaked space, further extending the room's apparent size.

■ **A PAINTED ARMOIRE** recedes visually since it is the same color as the walls.

■ **TWO EASY CHAIRS** are slipcovered in white to keep the look clean and airy. A voile cover on the round table gives it a light, ethereal quality.

MAKING THE MOST OF YOUR SPACE

# An Attic Retreat

Privacy in a busy household is just a staircase away. Create a sunny and secluded bedroom suite in the found space of a converted attic.

The top floor of a hotel or luxury apartment building is often considered the most desirable because of its privacy and prime views. When looking for space to locate a master bedroom, an attic is a wonderful option. By opening up your attic and filling it with light, you're not only making the most of your home's space, you also gain top-floor status for your private retreat.

The keys to a livable attic space are height and light. You need sufficient height to function comfortably, and as much daylight as possible to make the space energizing. Dormers are an invaluable addition because they increase both space and brightness. Windows and skylights brighten a room's interior and can make it appear larger than its actual dimensions. Look for any opportunity to add them, and consider nonstandard locations and unusual shapes. Once you have the room's structure in place, sticking with a focused color palette keeps it looking simple, open, and spacious.

## WHY THIS ROOM WORKS

A simple decorating approach allows this bedroom to make its own distinct mark while being open to the rest of the space.

■ A WOODEN POST AND BEAM subtly divide the sleeping area from office space. Support posts create an implied hallway between bed and workspace.

■ NEUTRAL-TONED FURNISHINGS, like the upholstered headboard and slipcovered chair, preserve a sense of spaciousness. Colorful accents pack extra punch against a backdrop of black, white, and neutrals.

■ SIMPLE BEDDING keeps the bed looking neat and is easy to make up.

■ DARK WOOD FLOORING grounds and warms up the space and unifies the sleeping and working areas.

MAKING THE MOST OF YOUR SPACE

# Wide-Open Space

If you've got a lot of space and want to celebrate it, remember: less is more. Keeping a large space simple emphasizes its openness.

Living in an open-plan room presents a different set of challenges around use of space. You may have so much of it that it's difficult to achieve separation between one area and the next. One option is to section off space with partial walls or large furniture pieces. Another is to use structural markers like columns or beams to subtly define boundaries and provide visual separation.

The great appeal of a space without divisions is its openness, so indulge in that sense of wide-open space. Choose sizable furniture pieces that suit the scale of the room and "float" them away from the walls for a serene effect. Add a few well-chosen accent pieces whose shapes complement the space. In an open-plan room, the sleeping area can often be seen from other areas, so it should look neat and be easy to maintain. Dressing the bed in neutral colors enhances the feeling of simplicity and calm, and lets you bring in bursts of color through pillows and other accessories.

CREATIVE DISPLAYS AND
CLEVER STORAGE FIND
A HOME IN THE UNUSED
SPACE AT THE FOOT OF
YOUR BED.

**A console table**, *left*, typically used in a living room, is often the right length and height to fit neatly at the end of a bed. Here, the decorative red boxes and plaid fabric runner echo the bedding, so the piece appears perfectly suited for the room.

**Wooden benches**, *above and top middle*, offer space for holding small baskets and boxes on top and underneath, expanding the room's storage possibilities. Benches are also a place to drape extra blankets at bedside, and they provide a convenient seat for dressing. The light pine bench (above) holds accessories and serves as a dressing table – an especially welcome touch for guest bedrooms.

**Two end tables**, *top right*, can act as one long storage unit at the foot of the bed. A stack of books fills the space between, and a fabric runner draped across the top unites them. Baskets holding magazines slide under each table.

**A folding table**, *right*, offers a moveable platform for bedside storage and display. In a guest bedroom, the table can be used as a luggage rack.

One of the greatest compliments a host can receive is hearing that overnight guests would like to return for another visit. That kind of encouragement makes having guests a great pleasure. Whether you're redoing a room or want to fit guest quarters into one that's used for another function, the first step is establishing a sense of privacy. Give visitors a space they can feel at home in. Make sure that even in a dual-use room, there's space for guests to unpack and claim an area as their own.

# WELCOMING
# HOUSEGUESTS

WHAT REALLY MATTERS TO GUESTS ARE SIMPLE PLEASURES. A PERFECT GUEST ROOM PROVIDES PRIVACY AND COMFORT, THEN ADDS TOUCHES THAT MAKE VISITORS FEEL SPECIAL.

Then, focus on the quality and comfort of the bed, choosing the best you're able to afford. Particularly if guests will be using a convertible sofa, test it yourself to ensure that the mattress is comfortable enough for a good night's sleep. Dress the bed in layers of fine fabrics that make guests feel pampered, and add small amenities to amplify a sense of welcome. A basket of muffins, a plush throw, a crystal pitcher of ice water, fresh new bars of special soap, and extra towels, blankets, and pillows – thoughtful accents are the mark of a gracious host. For a final touch, don't forget fresh flowers. Even one simple bud can soothe the senses.

# An Open Invitation

Planning for guests' needs is the cornerstone of good hospitality. Create a space for visitors that you'd also enjoy escaping to yourself.

If you're fortunate enough to have space for dedicated guest quarters in a bonus room, studio, or cottage, you're in a perfect position for hosting visiting friends and family. Create a quiet hideaway that's ready to welcome visitors at a moment's notice by keeping it well-stocked and full of comforting amenities.

Approach the room's design as you might if it were a studio apartment. Think beyond a comfortable bed. Plan for places to eat breakfast, write a letter, or curl up with a book in the afternoon. Then fill the armoire or closet with lots of blankets and bed linens, pillows, throws, towels, and bathrobes. Include an electric kettle and a basket of teas to make guests feel more at home.

## WHY THIS ROOM WORKS

Set up to be both a getaway for the homeowners and a self-sufficient guest room, this airy space gives visitors the feeling of having their own private cottage.

■ A COMFORTABLE DAYBED is a good choice for guest quarters since it doubles as a spot for relaxing, reading, or napping during the day.

■ A PEDESTAL TABLE presents a cozy spot for breakfast in the morning, provides a place to write a note or postcard at midday, and at night serves as a nightstand.

■ AN ARMOIRE offers generous storage for linens and bathrobes and leaves plenty of room for guests' clothing.

■ A STACK OF HATBOXES doubles as a charming bedside table and can be pressed into service for storage.

■ BEAUTIFUL TEXTILES — cotton bedding, a matelassé quilt, a linen tablecloth, and a shag rug — provide pleasure and comfort.

# The Gift of Serenity

An atmosphere of serenity is one of the most desirable assets a guest room can have. To create a calm retreat, furnish the space simply.

When traveling, sometimes the greatest luxury is a quiet place to rest. When planning a guest room, take a cue from gracious resorts and create a soothing, spa-like environment. Combine simple furnishings with high-quality luxurious fabrics and accessories inspired by nature to put a focus on reflective repose.

Start with the bedding. Rather than overdressing the bed, choose one or two covers in neutral colors that are crafted from invitingly tactile fabrics. Keep the room's furnishings spare and its color palette soft, then add just one or two notes of stronger color – perhaps an exotic flower or a decorative bottle of lotion – to gently punctuate the calm tone of the room.

## WHY THIS ROOM WORKS

Guests find refuge in this bedroom's peaceful, cloistered quality. Furnishings are simple and serene, and accents have been chosen to reinforce the setting's air of calm.

■ A WALL-MOUNTED SHELF softened with a fabric runner holds bedside amenities, eliminating the need for a nightstand and giving the bedside area greater apparent space.

■ TEXTURED BEDDING and a hand-quilted coverlet bring focus to the comfort of the bed.

■ A RUSTIC WOOD BENCH provides a simple spot to sit while dressing. Its unadorned style reinforces the pure simplicity of the decor.

■ A SINGLE BLOSSOM set in a bowl with floating candles further enhances the serene mood. Candles are used throughout the room to warm the space, and incense infuses the air.

■ A FEW UNDERSTATED ACCESSORIES give the room a finished look while maintaining its aesthetic.

# Cottage Comfort

Offer guests a welcome change from the workaday world with a room that recaptures the simple charms of a summer lodge.

Think of a favorite lakeside cabin or beach house you enjoyed staying in long ago. Its pleasures were likely not about luxury but rather were related to cool breezes and catnaps on a rumpled bed, fragrant with the fresh scents of the outdoors. When you have guests coming to stay, help them cast off their cares by inviting them into a room that renounces any notions of fussiness and re-creates those feelings of easy comfort.

To import the unembellished cheer of a summer room into your space, start with a clean slate. An all-white background not only evokes the look of warm-weather whitewashing, it also affords the greatest ability to change its appearance with a quick switch of bedding or accents. For furnishings, stick with the basics. A room free of clutter is many people's idea of heaven, so a comfortable bed, a modest nightstand, and a suitable lamp are the only essentials. Crisp bedding in bright colors adds instant appeal and completes the theme.

## WHY THIS ROOM WORKS

Bright sunshine, whitewashed walls, and crisp bed linens are all that's needed to provide pleasure in this cheerful room whose picturesque charms recall summers at the lake.

■ **WHITE WALLS AND FLOORS** create a clean, refreshing background that reflects natural light and makes the room feel more spacious.

■ **PATTERNED FABRICS** like the gingham-check sheets, matelassé quilt, and jacquard throw add inviting visual texture. Physical and visual textures are both especially important in a room that uses a lot of white, since texture more than color supplies visual interest.

■ **A HEMSTITCH BED SKIRT** recalls a time when heirloom linens were reserved for special guests.

■ **PAINTED PANELING WALLS** evoke the look and feel of a vacation home's sleeping porch.

■ **ACCENT PIECES** are kept to a minimum and stay within the red-and-white color scheme.

# BATHING

"TO ME, THE BATH IS

THE ULTIMATE RETREAT.

IT SHOULD BE PRIVATE AND

SOOTHING, FILLED WITH

REFRESHING AMENITIES

AND PLEASURES THAT

ENGAGE ALL OF MY SENSES."

ELEMENTS OF A SUCCESSFUL

# BATHROOM

More than ever before, a bathroom's decor can reflect the style and comfort of the rest of your home. Bathrooms were once hardworking no-frills zones – attractive, but functional first and foremost. These days, functionality remains important, of course. But the way we think about the bath has changed tremendously, and so much more is possible. A growing desire for balance in our lives means that the bath has become a larger part of our floor plans. It's now a room to spend time in – a space not only for cleansing but also for rest and contemplation. The rooms in the following pages show just a sampling of what's possible when creating a bathroom that's filled with light, warmth, and comfort.

# How to Plan a Bathroom

When planning an up-to-date bathroom for your home, take the space you have to work with and see how you can accommodate your decorating preferences. With so many options, a wish list is a good place to start.

In the bath perhaps more than in any other room, the best arrangement can be determined by noticing how you use the space. A lot can be learned about making your bathroom more functional and comfortable, even if you're not building a new one from scratch, and many furnishings or fittings can be added without major remodeling. For at least a week, pay attention to how you use your existing bath. Make a list of the things you'd do differently if you could. Do you see the bathroom as the one place you can escape to for

time alone, or do you enjoy sharing it with the whole family? If you like lingering here and you're able to splurge on new fixtures, a soaking tub offers the ultimate spa-like escape, and a double-size stall with tempered glass walls makes showering a whole new experience. But for a similar effect without a large contractor's bill, simply bring in a comfortable chair or chaise, have a steam shower or deluge showerhead fitted, or install custom lighting for reading in the tub. Similarly, look at your other needs and desires — for storage, lighting, and decoration — and realize that your options range from rebuilding to simply switching out the towels and shower curtain. Even small changes here can have a big impact. Compile your wish list based on thoughtful evaluation of day-to-day use, then enjoy exploring the decorating possibilities.

### THE ULTIMATE BATH

This sizable bath (above and preceding page) typifies a new approach to bath design. Used for rejuvenation as well as bathing, it incorporates furnishings from other rooms of the home.

■ A FREESTANDING BATHTUB is an increasingly popular choice in today's bathrooms. This installation highlights the tub's sculptural shape.

■ GRAND WINDOWS, such as those you might find in a living room, wash the room in natural sunlight.

■ A WOODEN VANITY TABLE introduces natural texture and warmth to the room, offsetting the cool white surfaces. Baskets and plants add further texural interest.

■ A CHAISE LONGUE provides a cozy spot to linger and enjoy the sun and solitude.

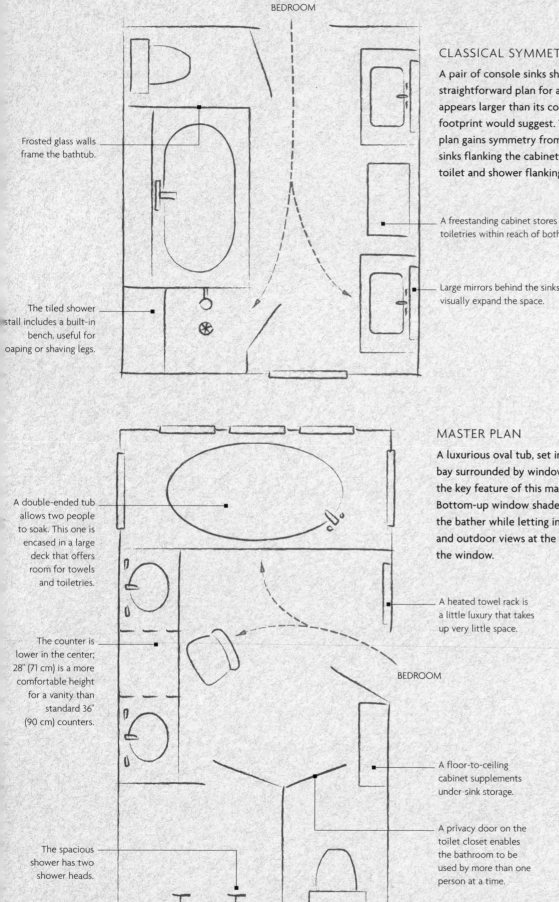

BEDROOM

## CLASSICAL SYMMETRY

A pair of console sinks shapes this straightforward plan for a bath that appears larger than its compact footprint would suggest. The floor plan gains symmetry from the two sinks flanking the cabinet and the toilet and shower flanking the tub.

Frosted glass walls frame the bathtub.

A freestanding cabinet stores toiletries within reach of both sinks.

Large mirrors behind the sinks visually expand the space.

The tiled shower stall includes a built-in bench, useful for soaping or shaving legs.

## MASTER PLAN

A luxurious oval tub, set into a bay surrounded by windows, is the key feature of this master bath. Bottom-up window shades screen the bather while letting in light and outdoor views at the top of the window.

A double-ended tub allows two people to soak. This one is encased in a large deck that offers room for towels and toiletries.

A heated towel rack is a little luxury that takes up very little space.

The counter is lower in the center; 28" (71 cm) is a more comfortable height for a vanity than standard 36" (90 cm) counters.

BEDROOM

A floor-to-ceiling cabinet supplements under-sink storage.

A privacy door on the toilet closet enables the bathroom to be used by more than one person at a time.

The spacious shower has two shower heads.

## SPACE REQUIREMENTS

Drawing a scale floor plan of your space will indicate how fixtures will fit into your room. You can try several different layouts until you arrive at one that best satisfies your needs. Work with the minimum dimensions below to allow ample room to move around.

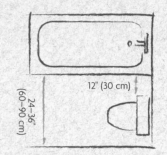

24–36" (60–90 cm)

12" (30 cm)

### Tub

Allow at least 12" (30 cm) between tub and an adjacent fixture, 24–36" (60–90 cm) between tub and a wall. A shower stall requires at least a 36" square (90 cm) space; also, allow room for the shower door to open fully.

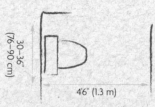

30–36" (76–90 cm)

4'6" (1.3 m)

### Toilet

A space of 4'6" (1.3 m) from the wall it is mounted on is needed for a toilet. Allow a width of 30–36" (76–90 cm).

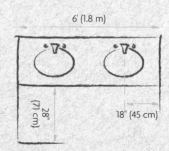

6' (1.8 m)

28" (71 cm)

18" (45 cm)

### Sinks

A minimum of 6' (1.8 m) of counter space is needed for two sinks. The center of a sink should be at least 18" (45 cm) from an adjoining wall. Allow a minimum of 28" (71 cm) clearance to stand and use the sink.

Perhaps no room in the house has changed more drastically than the bath. You need only look back a few decades to recall how small bathrooms used to be and how limited their options. Today, baths have significantly larger and more variable footprints, opening up more possibilities for how you configure your space and what you include. Beyond the basics, you can now include a double shower *and* a tub, dressing areas, walk-in closets, and even exercise equipment. You may want a "wet

# UPDATING
## THE CLASSIC BATH

NEW FIXTURES ARE JUST A STARTING POINT FOR REIMAGINING A BATH. THE NEW BATH IS ALL ABOUT COMFORT, SO MAKE YOURS AS SPLENDID AS ANY OTHER ROOM IN YOUR HOME.

room," where every surface is waterproof, or a stylish bathing space furnished with materials and furniture normally associated with other rooms in the house. Wooden armoires and chests of drawers, fine wood flooring, and comfortable reading chairs are now as at home here as in your living room or bedroom. The space that was formerly the home's most utilitarian is becoming its most personal, so it ought to reflect your spirit and style. As we increasingly view the bath as a natural extension of the rest of the home, we're taking it to new levels of luxury and comfort, and changing the very definition of what a bathroom can be.

## WHY THIS ROOM WORKS

This light-filled bath makes room for both functional pieces and decorative furnishings in its open, generous floor plan.

■ A WOODEN CONSOLE fitted with a marble countertop is typical of a new trend in baths. A creative use of furniture in the bathroom adds interest and individuality to the space.

■ A CLAW-FOOT BATHTUB soaks up the sun in the bay window, creating a dramatic focal point.

■ SEAMLESS GLASS on a double shower adds to the sense of the room's expansiveness.

■ AN ANTIQUE WOODEN BENCH and a zinc table help keep the room personal and warm, balancing the space's grand proportions.

UPDATING THE CLASSIC BATH

# A Spacious Plan

Free the bathroom from its traditional box by creating a light-filled room rich with architectural details and unique furnishings.

The trend of allotting more space for a bathroom is indicative of a growing recognition of the bath's importance in our lives as a space for rejuvenation. If you're fortunate enough to have a spacious bath, take advantage of its assets by flooding it with natural light and keeping it open and airy. In a room like this, a free-standing tub becomes a natural focal point, and positioning it near a window makes the most of the influx of light. Large windows, skylights, and even patio doors that open out to a garden are becoming increasingly common in today's baths.

Shower stalls also have become larger and more luxurious. To make the most of a roomy shower, use seamless glass walls instead of a curtain, which creates a sense of spaciousness even in a small room. Take advantage of the wide variety of fittings and configurations now available on the market, including "rain" shower heads, steam showers, and dual showers.

# The Wet Room

Break the boundaries of the traditional bath. Dispense with dividers and design a wide-open space that celebrates the joys of bathing.

In a true "wet room," all surfaces are waterproof and the space has a central floor drain, eliminating the need for an enclosed shower stall. Less structured and more freewheeling than a typical bathroom, wet rooms let you luxuriate completely in the pleasures of water.

You might also choose to create a partial wet room, waterproofing just the area within reach of the shower's spray. Either way, the floor should be sloped to a central drain to prevent water from pooling, and unpolished flooring materials such as slate are best chosen, as they offer more traction when wet than do smooth surfaces. It's also wise to plan for a dry zone in the room, so that towels and robes stay out of the spray.

## WHY THIS ROOM WORKS

In this beautifully practical room, surfaces are waterproof throughout the space. An absence of dividers or curtains lets water run freely and makes bathing a joy.

■ LARGE WINDOWS let in air and sunlight to help dry damp surfaces. Textured acrylic window panels are water-resistant and provide privacy. Above the sink, where a mirror is essential, windowpanes have cleverly been fitted with reflective glass.

■ A FREESTANDING TUB rests on a wide platform, which defines a shower area in the corner. A floor-mounted side faucet allows bathers to rest their heads comfortably at either end.

■ SLATE FLOORING is used throughout the room for a natural look and for enhanced traction underfoot.

■ STUCCO WALLS are treated with water resistant paint to protect them

■ SMOOTH RIVER ROCKS and starfish reinforce the water theme.

WHY THIS ROOM WORKS

Furnishings typically found in other rooms are at home here, making this a dreamy place to refresh. Sited in a summer house, the room's exposed framework adds a cottage-like charm.

■ **WET AND DRY ZONES** are defined by smart furniture placement. Separation is further emphasized with rugs – terry over crushed bamboo at the tub, plush pile in the seating area.

■ **A NETTING CANOPY** suggests romance and focuses attention on the striking freestanding tub.

■ **PLENTIFUL VENTILATION** helps this bath stay dry. Materials like cotton twill on the chair are bath-friendly, and the rustic wood surfaces are painted and sealed for protection.

UPDATING THE CLASSIC BATH

# A Furnished Bath

The new bath is more than a place for bathing. Furnish it with the comforts of a bedroom to create a romantic, personal space for relaxing.

When you have the luxury of space in a bath, transform the room into a private retreat by bringing in furniture, fabrics, and accessories that make you want to linger. Slipcovered furniture provides cozy spots for reading or unwinding (choose coverings in fabrics that are easy to change and wash such as twill, denim, chenille, terry cloth, or linen). Textured area rugs or patterned rugs like Orientals or kilims offer softness underfoot, and they also help delineate different areas. An armoire or dresser meant for the bedroom can provide much-needed storage in a bathroom as well, where its wood tones warm up a room full of otherwise cool materials. When bringing wood furniture into a bath, be sure it's painted or sealed to resist water.

In a furnished bath, it's important to create a floor plan that works well. A useful approach is to define zones for bathing, grooming, and lounging, allowing enough space between them so that nonbathing areas stay dry.

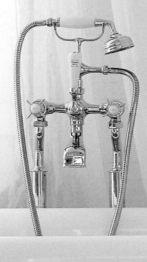

## WHY THIS ROOM WORKS

Traditional materials find new expression in this polished bath. Lustrous glass tile, sculptural sinks, stainless-steel counters, and natural wood combine to create a refined, contemporary space.

■ **GLASS MOSAIC TILES** have greater depth of color than conventional ceramic tiles, and are used here in an innovative way – floor-to-ceiling in the shower and in a decorative band behind the sinks.

■ **OPEN CABINETRY** is a stylish alternative to the traditional vanity.

■ **HIGH-STYLE FIXTURES AND FITTINGS** like the beautifully shaped vessel sinks and the single toggle-handled faucets reinforce the fashionable aesthetic.

■ **NATURAL WOOD**, sealed to protect against water damage, provides a warm contrast to the stainless steel and tile but retains a streamlined look.

UPDATING THE CLASSIC BATH

# Material Choices

With so many new options in materials, a bath can be tailored to any taste. Pair warm wood with cool metal and tile for a fresh, clean look.

Materials in the bathroom are by necessity chosen for functionality. With the array of choices currently available, there are also innumerable ways to showcase their beauty and combine them in surprising ways.

Tile has been used for centuries, but recent innovations in design and fabrication have made it more versatile than ever. Mosaic tiles, for example, are often used to give a bathroom a vintage look, especially tumbled stone or octagonal-shaped tiles. But when paired with up-to-date design elements – open wood cabinetry, stainless-steel counters, dramatic vessel sinks – mosaics look fashionably contemporary, particularly in newer styles like glass or metallic. Keep in mind that floor tiles in the bath must be slip-resistant, so some types won't be appropriate for bathroom flooring.

# Sinks and Faucets

Sinks are a major design element of the bath, and choices run the gamut from reproductions of classic styles to innovative new shapes. A sink may be a wall-mounted unit that takes up little space, or it can be set into the top of a cabinet that has storage space underneath. Vessel basins, mounted on top of a counter, are a newer option. You can use almost any sort of vessel as a sink as long as it can be plumbed. Pedestal sinks are another option and also come in a wide range of styles.

Fittings, or trim – bath terms that apply to faucets, handles, and other hardware – are as varied as sinks. Available materials include chrome, nickel, pewter, and stainless steel, all in polished, brushed, or matte finishes. Other options include the warm tones of brass, bronze, and copper. When choosing fittings, be sure the faucet spout is long enough to flow directly over the drain. See Materials, page 358, for more about sinks.

A sampling of faucets, *clockwise from top left,* shows the scope of styles available: a reproduction center-set faucet with lever handles; a classic English-style two-handle set with a teapot spout; a gooseneck faucet; and a wall-mounted faucet with single lever handle.

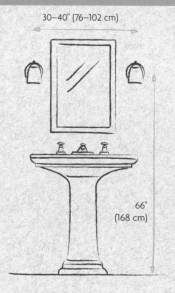

## DESIGN LESSON LIGHTING THE FACE

When choosing lighting at the bathroom sink or mirror, the goal is to provide enough light so that you can see clearly when applying makeup or shaving. If using fluorescent bulbs, be sure to choose full-spectrum; normal fluorescents can give skin unnatural tones. Halogen bulbs also provide crisp white light. Whatever fixtures you choose, use translucent lenses or shades with them; clear shades can cause glare, and opaque ones block too much light.

### Fixture Placement

To evenly light the face, a smart option is to mount fixtures at eye level, approximately 66" (168 cm) from the floor and about 30–40" (76–102 cm) apart. Lighting from both sides is a smart choice because light from above may cast unflattering shadows.

30–40" (76–102 cm)

66" (168 cm)

## Pedestal Sink

A classic bathroom fixture, a pedestal sink rests on a single column that partially conceals plumbing. Pedestal sinks give a bathroom a more spacious look because they take up less visual space than a vanity cabinet. Because pedestal styles don't offer the storage of vanity styles, be sure you have plenty of other storage options.

## Wall-Mounted Sink

A smart choice for small baths, a wall-mounted sink opens up floor space, creating the illusion of a larger room. The sink shown here is an updated interpretation. Its clever design encloses the plumbing and incorporates rods on which to hang hand towels. Look for a model with a wide deck around the bowl if you don't have a shelf or table nearby.

## Vessel Sink

With the striking look of a decorative object, this new sink style harks back to the classic Victorian china washbasin that sat on every nightstand. Vessel sinks elevate the bowl to a more comfortable height for washing, and work best when paired with wall-mounted fittings. They are available in a wide range of shapes and materials, including ceramic, metal, and glass.

## Corner Sink

This design is a great space saver, and, in some cases, the only style that will fit. Small corner sinks like this are a popular choice for powder rooms. Often, specialized sizes and shapes are available to solve awkward positioning problems. In this case, decorative moulding on the lower edge helps the sink blend in with the vintage-inspired bath.

## Console Sink

Consoles have two or four legs and support a deck with single or double sinks. Two-legged models rely on the wall for some support. Originally made popular as reproductions of antiques, console sinks are now available in contemporary styles, too, and often incorporate towel bars into their design. Antique models can usually be found at architectural salvage outlets.

## Washstand Sink

An antique washstand can be updated with modern plumbing to give period character to a bath. Here, a Victorian oak washstand with a marble slab deck and shelf was fitted to house two sinks. Wood furniture adds warmth to a bathroom but should be sealed for water resistance. A chest of drawers can also be fitted with a sink, but plumbing will take up some drawer space.

In the past, when the entire family shared one bathroom, it was a challenge to schedule grooming time. These days, many families have more space, but sharing is often still an issue. Everyone wants a bathing area that's tailored to their needs. Mom may want things one way and Dad another; if children are sharing, they have their own special requirements, as do houseguests. If it's not feasible to give each person their own separate vanity and sink, there are still solutions for allowing

# ENJOYING
## A SHARED BATHROOM

SHARING A BATHROOM IS A PLEASURE WHEN YOU'VE PLANNED FOR EVERYONE'S NEEDS. MAKE EACH FAMILY MEMBER AND GUEST FEEL COMFORTABLY CARED FOR.

everyone a sense of their own space. Towel bars are easy to install, so assign one to each user — a great first step in making everyone feel cared for. Zone the room for maximum personalization and privacy, and plan storage that offers a place for everyone's individual items. Built-in cabinets are the most customizable and can range from a simple, cleverly divided undersink vanity to deluxe his-and-hers dressing areas; shelving is another flexible storage option that can be added to most rooms. Finally, make the bath both pleasant and practical by stocking lots of basic necessities like towels and tissue and finding attractive ways to display them.

WHY THIS ROOM WORKS

As well-planned as it is visually pleasing, this bright vintage-style bathroom is an up-to-date haven for two to enjoy morning or night.

- **BANKS OF WINDOWS** surround the tub and brighten the entire room. Tailored linen shades offer privacy.

- **HANDSOME NICKEL SCONCES** flank the twin mirrors, offering balanced light for day or evening.

- **A SHALLOW CABINET** provides useful storage around the pedestal sinks. The 12"-deep (30 cm) cabinet not only makes space for drawers but also provides a tiled shelf for toiletries.

- **SHELVES ABOVE THE TUB** create a spot for a music system and small TV that can be viewed while in the tub.

ENJOYING A SHARED BATHROOM

# Side-by-Side Style

Sharing a bathroom is sometimes a favored choice. Couples can enjoy starting or ending a day together in a space that's built for comfort.

In busy households, the master bath is often a main communication center where you preview the day's schedule or catch up at night after the kids are in bed. You need a bathroom that's bright and invigorating to start the day yet subdued and soothing at its end.

Equip the room to spend time in it. A music system, a small TV for the morning news, and an easy chair or chaise all help add to the comfort of a shared space. Keep candles, matches, and calming fragrances on hand so you'll be more likely to use them daily.

Nothing is better for energy than natural light, so uncover as many windows as possible and supplement daylight with lamps at the mirror, to evenly light the face for applying makeup or shaving. Flexible lighting can also deliver a more atmospheric effect at night. To subdue the lighting for evening, put overhead fixtures on a different switch from vanity lights, and use dimmers for all switches to give you greater control.

# The Master Bath

Share your bath and enjoy the company. Make your master bathroom a stylish space that offers both togetherness and privacy.

If you share your bathroom with a mate but crave the comforts of a private domain, take the old his-and-hers concept to its new, luxurious conclusion. Create tailor-made spaces for each user that include not only individual sinks but also separate grooming areas, closets, and dressing areas. Allow space for storage of personal items near each sink or vanity, and keep shared supplies in a place convenient to both users. As in any room, a continuity of style is necessary for visual unity; look to the rest of your home for ideas and inspiration to make your bath into a retreat that's as stylish as any other room. Incorporating comfortable seating and fine materials like hardwood flooring and decorative paneling gives a bathroom unexpected sophistication.

## WHY THIS ROOM WORKS

Designed for a couple, this generous master bathroom caters to each person's needs with separate his-and-hers areas for bathing, grooming, and dressing.

■ CUSTOMIZED ZONES are dedicated to each person — a vanity table for her, a chest of drawers for him.

■ A WINDOW SEAT offers a handy place to put on socks and shoes or a spot to rest after a hot bath.

■ A DEEP FREESTANDING TUB with a side-mounted faucet is spacious enough for two to share comfortably.

■ NATURAL LIGHT, from a window over the vanity table, is ideal for applying makeup.

■ SOPHISTICATED MATERIALS, including decorative mouldings, dark wood countertops, and hardwood floors, warm the room's white palette.

■ A PARTITIONED ALCOVE for the toilet provides privacy.

## WHY THIS ROOM WORKS

Every inch of space is maximized in this neat family bathroom. Good planning makes room for everyone's things, from toiletries and towels to kids' bath toys.

■ A DOUBLE-SIDED CABINET divides the room for privacy and houses storage that's accessible from both sides. Shallow shelves for toiletries open to the sink side; deeper shelving for towels faces the tub.

■ PLASTIC BUCKETS are a practical and attractive storage solution for kids' bath necessities. A small stool helps youngsters get in and out of the tub and allows Mom to sit while young ones bathe.

■ A BUILT-IN LAUNDRY CHUTE is a smart detail that helps keep the space tidy and organized.

■ PERSONALIZED HOOKS make sure that everyone knows where to find his or her towel after bathing.

ENJOYING A SHARED BATHROOM

# The Family Bath

Careful planning, creative furnishing, and plenty of storage contribute to making a family bath a pleasure to share.

A shared bathroom requires creative planning to comfortably accommodate the comings and goings of an entire family. The key is organization. One great option for storage is a unit that can double as a privacy screen or room divider. By making shelving accessible from two sides, you maximize its capacity. Each family member then has easy access to his or her own toiletries, and there's still plenty of room for basic bathroom necessities. If young children use the room, systems must be straightforward and easy to understand. Big buckets or bins and towel hooks with name tags let little ones know just where things should go. Empty walls, especially above the toilet, offer potential shelving space for additional storage, as does hallway space just outside the room, where additional cabinets may fit.

A bathroom that anticipates guests' needs gives them an inviting place to relax. Wainscoting on the walls and antique-style fittings give the room a period look.

■ **AN EN-SUITE SETUP** is ideal for guest quarters, allowing visitors to have their own space filled with just-for-them amenities.

■ **BOUTIQUE-HOTEL TOUCHES** like fine toiletries and fresh bathrobes transform even a simple room.

■ **VINTAGE-STYLE CONTAINERS** hold decanted bath gel, shampoo, and conditioner; fresh hand-milled guest soaps add luxury.

■ **A STACK OF TOWELS**, a new pair of slippers, and some fresh-cut greenery show the kind of personal attention that makes guests feel pampered.

■ **A NEUTRAL PALETTE** is a soothing backdrop that makes accents stand out and lets you adapt the room's look to the changing seasons.

ENJOYING A SHARED BATHROOM

# Guest Appearances

Small amenities and thoughtful details are an easy way to say "welcome" when preparing a guest bath for visiting friends and relatives.

Sharing your home with houseguests is a pleasure that's easy to enjoy when you've planned for it. Focusing on the details in a guest bath makes even a small space seem sumptuous. Stock the room with the kinds of amenities that you might find in a plush hotel – fine toiletries like aromatherapy soaps, shampoos, and bath gel, and stacks of fluffy towels. Anticipate guests' needs by providing hard-to-pack items like a hairdryer and thick, cozy bathrobes. Keep everything in plain sight so that guests are able to find things easily. Remember, too, that visitors will need space to put out their own belongings, so make room in the medicine cabinet and on counters or shelves for them. Finally, add flowers or greenery to give the space fresh appeal.

INDULGE YOUR GUESTS WITH
THOUGHTFUL TOUCHES AND SIMPLE,
LUXURIOUS AMENITIES THAT MAKE
THEM FEEL WELL CARED FOR.

**Handsome containers**, *left*, a few well-selected toiletries, and a fresh orchid stem are the kinds of grace notes you'd find in a fine hotel. Amenities don't have to be lavish to make guests feel special.

**Glass cake domes**, *above*, showcase a tempting array of lotions, soaps, and colognes. An assortment of toiletries, presented creatively, gives guests the pleasure of sampling new products, which you can let them take home as gifts.

**Gardenia blossoms**, *above right*, in a wooden box lend their sweet scent to the bath; guests can toss flowers into their bathwater for a relaxing soak. Fresh flowers are one of the most appreciated accents in a guest room.

**Men's grooming essentials**, *right*, are arranged on vintage pewter trays. Trays are a convenient way to present guest amenities, because the entire collection can be easily moved or stored away.

Few people have the pleasure of visiting a spa every day, but you can come close in your own home bath. Historically, a visit to a spa was known as "taking the waters," and water is still key to a spa experience, from mineral baths to Vichy showers. At home, deluxe fixtures like soaking tubs, which allow bathing immersed up to your chin, offer a spa-like indulgence in water. Most spa treatments end with a quiet rest, so a cozy chair or chaise longue is an especially sumptuous addition to

# REFRESHING
## BODY AND SOUL

SPAS ARE DEDICATED TO REJUVENATING BODY AND SPIRIT. RECREATE A SPA EXPERIENCE AT HOME WITH A BATH DESIGNED TO DELIGHT THE SENSES.

your own bathroom. If you have less room to work with, your resting spot might be as simple as a sauna-like bench softened with piles of pillows. What's most important is making your surroundings as tranquil and pleasing to the senses as possible. Aim for a purity of space and furnishing that promotes serenity. Open the room to sunlight and views to the outdoors. Choose a restful color palette, perhaps taking inspiration from water or nature. Enjoy the benefits of aromatherapy with bath infusions, fresh flowers, or candles, and keep stacks of plush towels at hand. Stock soothing lotions and other amenities that make you feel pampered.

# An At-Home Spa

Treat yourself to the ultimate bath experience. Incorporating a deep soaking tub into your bathroom turns it into your own home spa.

In Japan, bathing is not something one does just to cleanse the body. It is a centuries-old ritual used to rejuvenate both body and spirit. A deep tub, called an *ofuro*, is filled with steaming hot water for soaking; cleansing takes place separately, prior to entering the ofuro. Many people spend at least half an hour each evening soaking in a tub, contemplating the day.

Fortunately, you don't need to go to Japan to relax. Soaking tubs are now widely available for home baths (see pages 237 and 361). Custom-built tubs can be made in any size, usually from cedar, redwood, or teak. Ready-made models, both freestanding and drop-in, are available in acrylic, fiberglass, metal, and wood.

## WHY THIS ROOM WORKS

As aesthetically pleasing as it is physically comforting, this serene home spa with its traditional Japanese soaking tub soothes the senses in every way.

■ A CEDAR SOAKING TUB filled with steaming water is roomy enough for several people to share. The platform is a traditional Japanese design and offers the warmth of natural wood.

■ CANDLES AND INCENSE scent the room. Soothing herbal bath infusions and aromatherapy oils are also at hand to enhance comfort.

■ A BUILT-IN BENCH and plenty of pillows provide a space for lounging, chatting, or meditating. A chaise longue offers a comfortable spot to stretch out before or after soaking.

■ NATURAL MATERIALS used throughout the room are practical, pleasing, and bath-friendly.

■ WALLS OF WINDOWS make nature an integral part of the setting.

# Natural Senses

Bring the serenity of a spa to your own bath with simple, sculptural shapes and a pleasing organic palette of colors and materials.

One way to bring spa style to a bathroom is by using an economy of ornament and opting for an elemental aesthetic. Choose simple fixtures and fittings, and pair them with colors, materials, and accents drawn from nature, to give a bath the feel of a luxurious retreat.

As with any furnishings in your home, simple pieces focus on purity of shape and contribute to a sense of spaciousness. Wall-mounted sinks leave floor space open below them; flush-mounted cabinets keep the wall plane unbroken; freestanding tubs' graceful forms may appear less massive than built-ins. Complement this streamlined approach with natural materials like terra-cotta or stone, and bring in fresh greenery for accents.

## WHY THIS ROOM WORKS

This city sanctuary is made luxurious with spa-style simplicity. Muted earth tones are a calming backdrop for crisp white fixtures and fresh green accents.

■ AN ACRYLIC SOAKING TUB in a striking contemporary shape serves as the centerpiece of the room.

■ SIMPLY DESIGNED FIXTURES and furnishings — wall-mounted sinks, flush-mounted wall cabinets, a unique sculptural toilet — establish the room's quiet aesthetic.

■ SALTILLO FLOOR TILES are a sensual treat for feet and lend an earthy character to the room, grounding the high-style fixtures.

■ GLASS MOSAIC TILES wrapping the walls and ceiling of the shower stall give it a luminous quality.

■ POTTED PLANTS thrive in the humid bath environment and contribute to the spa atmosphere. Scented blooming plants are especially soothing.

**Handheld Shower**, *right*
Nostalgia for early-20th-century bath fittings has spawned reproductions with modern functionality. This period set combines a tub-filler faucet, crossbar handles, and a handheld shower, as well as a conventional showerhead at the top of the exposed vertical pipe.

**Floor-Mounted Fittings**, *far right* Faucets that are mounted on the floor and situated at the center of the tub allow bathers to lean back in comfort at either end of the tub. With the increased popularity of double-ended tubs, this configuration is becoming more and more common.

**Deluge Showerhead**, *right*
This circular showerhead style – also known as a rain or sunflower showerhead – simulates the feeling of an overhead downpour. Available in a variety of sizes, the sensation it delivers is an invigorating way to start the day. Bear in mind that these styles use more water than a conventional showerhead and so require a larger water-heater capacity.

**Dual-Control Mixers**, *far right* Shower mixers, like this classic Victorian design, have separate flow and temperature controls. Mixers in contemporary styles are also widely available

# Tubs and Fittings

When selecting a bathtub, size is a dual concern: a tub needs to fit the dimensions of your space, and it also must accommodate the dimensions of your body. Currently, standard-size tubs are 60 inches (152 cm) long and 32 inches (81 cm) wide, but you can find shorter models, or longer and deeper ones, in many styles.

While available floor space clearly plays a part in selecting a tub, your preferences for the type of installation and the look it gives the bathroom are also important. Freestanding tubs, such as the perennial favorite claw-foot, require a bit more space but offer flexibility because they can be positioned anywhere in the room. Built-in tubs are also classic, and they're increasingly being skirted in wood, tile, or stone to make them appear more like furniture. The fittings that you choose (see opposite) should complement your tub but don't have to be the exact same style. For more information on tubs, see Materials, page 361.

**Bathtub styles,** *clockwise from top left,* a classic rolltop tub with a wood skirt and marble deck; an Empire-style freestanding tub with floor-mounted fittings; a whirlpool tub with tinted concrete surround; and a freestanding reproduction claw-foot tub.

## DESIGN LESSON ADDING A SOAKING TUB

A luxurious new option in bath design has made its way from the spa into residential bathrooms: the soaking tub. These tubs are at least several inches deeper than conventional ones, allowing you to fully immerse yourself for a more relaxing experience. Just like other tubs, they come in a variety of shapes, sizes, and materials, from enameled cast iron to acrylic, ceramic, copper, vinyl, or wood. The defining feature is depth. Most are a standard 20–22" (51–56 cm) deep, as compared to 14–16" (36–41 cm) in a conventional tub. Some models, styled after Japanese ofuro soaking tubs (see page 232), allow you to sit upright in the water and can be as deep as 34" (86 cm). Many designs also offer whirlpool options.

There are several factors to keep in mind if you're thinking of incorporating a soaking tub into your bathroom.

■ WATER CAPACITY It can take 60–75 gallons (227–284 l) of water to fill a standard soaking tub (compared to about 42 gallons/159 l for an ordinary standard tub), so make sure your water heater has the capacity to provide that much hot water efficiently.

■ WEIGHT Eighty gallons of water weighs about 667 pounds (303 kg). The tub itself can run from 125 pounds (57 kg) for acrylic to up to 500 pounds (227 kg) for an enameled cast-iron tub. Make sure your flooring structure can support the weight.

WORKIN

"MY HOME OFFICE NEEDS
TO BE CREATIVE AS
WELL AS FUNCTIONAL.
I WANT THIS SPACE TO BE
A SOURCE OF NEW IDEAS
AND FRESH INSPIRATION
FOR EVERY PROJECT."

# HOME OFFICE

It used to be that "home" and "office" were concepts as separate and opposite as one could imagine, and we worked hard to keep things that way. Nowadays, the lines are less distinct, and many of us work at home at least part of the time. Make your home a place where you can get work done, and make your office a place that feels like home. Designing a workspace that's an integrated part of your house and in harmony with its decor is a win-win situation. A handsome home office encourages productivity while still offering home-style comfort. In this chapter, we've chosen a few of our favorite spaces to show you, to help you imagine what's possible in creating a great workspace.

# How to Plan a Home Office

When planning the layout of your home office, learn from the concept of the kitchen work triangle, which allows for the most efficient use of space. An L-shaped, U-shaped, or galley arrangement puts everything within easy reach.

Wherever your office may be, you'll find work easier to organize if you have two principal work areas: one in front of the computer and another for doing phone- and paperwork. Plan, too, for easy access to file storage, your printer/fax/copier, and daily supplies. With a compact L- or U-shaped layout, you can pivot from one area to the other easily. The same is true for a galley setup, where you sit between parallel work surfaces. The way you want your office to appear to visitors also influences decisions on its arrangement. For instance, an L-shaped workstation may leave you and your paperwork on view to guests or clients, whereas a galley allows you to stow ongoing work in a cabinet that sits behind you. Store things that you use on a daily basis (phone, files, pens, clips, staplers, and so on) within arm's reach, no more than 3 feet (90 cm) away from the side of your chair. Less-used items and archival records are better stored outside of your immediate work area.

Remember to include space for displaying things that are comforting and inspiring to you – not just family photographs but also art and decorative objects, perhaps related to your business or avocation. An "inspiration board" can boost your creative energy; fill it with postcards, magazine clippings, and work that you admire. Also, be sure to include an easy chair so you can review papers in comfort or simply relax and take a break.

## AN ORDERLY L-SHAPED OFFICE

This office (above and preceding page) takes up little floor space and defines its work areas with linear storage. This compact setup could fit onto a landing or in another small space.

■ A CONSISTENT STYLE of office furniture creates a sense of order, and individual units offer specialized storage. A corner desk area is included for computer work, and another desk bay is available for paperwork.

■ A BULLETIN-BOARD UNIT is a valuable information center that holds a calendar, important notes, and inspirational images.

■ DAYLIGHT makes any workspace more pleasant, but windows can create glare, so position the computer monitor so that light strikes it from the side.

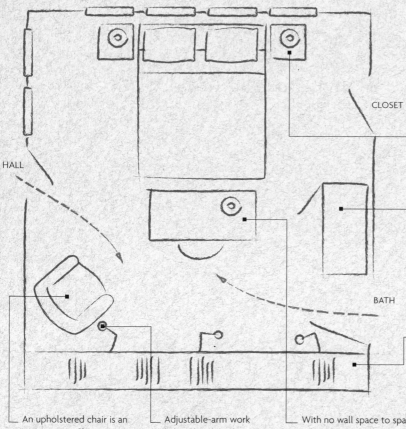

## IN A GUEST BEDROOM

Because a guest room is used only occasionally, it makes good sense to take advantage of the space for use as an office. Plan concealed storage that allows you to quickly clean up.

CLOSET

A pair of attractive wooden file cabinets are used as nightstands — a clever way to introduce dual-use pieces into the room.

HALL

A cabinet or armoire can be customized with special storage systems to keep business equipment and supplies out of sight. It also offers space for guests to store their belongings.

BATH

A wall of shelves provides generous storage for books and files. Use boxes and baskets to organize loose items among the shelves.

An upholstered chair is an asset in any office, providing a comfortable place to read and review work; it's also a nice amenity for guests.

Adjustable-arm work lights clip onto the shelves, providing accent lighting and visual warmth.

With no wall space to spare, a small desk fits neatly at the foot of the bed; an extension cord runs under the bed to power a desk lamp.

## A DEDICATED WORKSPACE

An extra bedroom is well suited for conversion into a home office that uses a wall of closets as its primary storage space. Choose a desk and comfortable chairs from a home furnishings store rather than an office supply store, to better complement the rest of the home's interiors.

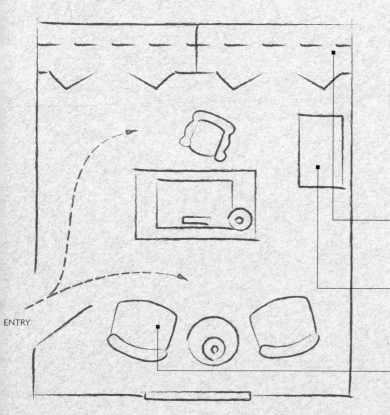

ENTRY

Opt for lateral file cabinets, which are only 18" (45 cm) deep and so fit easily into a standard closet.

A separate worktable has shelving built in below. It offers a place to keep files, papers, and other day-to-day necessities at hand.

Comfortable chairs are a must for clients and also allow you to take a break.

## OFFICE COMFORT

You're more productive when you are comfortable, and that includes everything from computer height to sufficient lighting (lighting for desk work is addressed on page 351). Use this checklist for positioning office furniture.

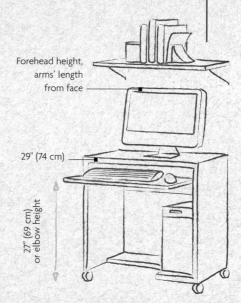

Forehead height, arms' length from face

29" (74 cm)

27" (69 cm) or elbow height

**Computer Screen**
Your monitor should be directly in front of you with the screen at arm's length and the top of the screen no higher than your forehead.

**Keyboard**
Though standard desk height is 29" (74 cm), most people are more comfortable typing with their hands at about 27" (69 cm). To determine the best height for you, sit in a desk chair with your arms bent at your sides; the keyboard should be at the height of your elbows.

**Desk**
A minimum space of 30" (76 cm) square is needed for most desk work, adequate for a computer screen, phone, and letter-size papers. Allow at least 3' (90 cm) of clearance behind the desk for a chair.

**Worktable**
A small worktable on casters, about 26" (66 cm) high, is a handy addition. Use it to hold files and supplies you'll need for the day, or use it as your computer station to keep your main desk clear.

Once you've decided to claim a space for an office in your home, you need to make it workable. More to the point, you need to make it work *for you*. What does your ideal workspace look like? There are basic elements that apply to almost any room, of course, like smart space planning, sufficient lighting, and adequate storage. But which choices can you make to create an office that is inspirational as well as functional? First, find the right space in your home, whether an attic retreat or a corner

# DESIGNING A
# HOME OFFICE

TO CREATE AN IDEAL WORKSPACE, TRUST YOUR INTUITION. FIND THE COLORS, FURNISHINGS, AND TYPES OF SPACES THAT PLEASE YOU, AND LET THEM GUIDE YOUR DESIGN.

of the kitchen. Then, make sure it's efficiently planned and comfortably furnished. Think about whether you prefer traditional furniture or creative alternatives: a classic desk, or a sheet of wood set across file cabinets? Pay attention to which colors you respond to, how much light you like, and which little extras give you a sense of luxury, and let these details inform your design choices. Storage figures prominently here, and one of the keys to a smart-looking office space is keeping it clutter-free. Remember that you're at home, though: think beyond the file cabinet, and find imaginative or whimsical alternatives to standard office pieces.

WHY THIS ROOM WORKS

Once a dim and dusty attic, this bright, uncluttered office for two architects started with a clean canvas of white walls and ceilings.

■ **THREE ADJOINING TABLES** in the center of the work area provide stations for two people plus a large surface for presentations that's accessible from all sides.

■ **A CENTRAL STAIRWELL** divides the attic into work and storage areas.

■ **A SKYLIGHT** brings natural light into this space with few windows.

■ **RECESSED LIGHTING** is concealed by pieces of wood, and exposed rafters create an open feeling.

■ **PLEXIGLAS-TOPPED TABLES** manage the potential clutter of work clippings and inspirational photos.

DESIGNING A HOME OFFICE

# An Attic Office

If you need space for an office, a roomy attic is a top-flight option. Create an airy workspace that's high above the bustle of home.

An underused attic may prove to be a hidden treasure when you're looking for office space. Attics often have plenty of space that you can put into service, and they offer a romantic sense of being in a creative hideout.

If your attic is currently an unfinished space, several key issues should be addressed before transforming it into a work area. You'll need to make sure that ceiling height and floor support are sufficient, and that your electrical capacity can handle the day-to-day demands. Consult with a licensed professional, too, about insulation and venting, as attic temperatures can affect your comfort as well as your office equipment's ability to function.

Once you get the go-ahead, remember that in a small enclosed room, less is more. Bathing the space in light (skylights are ideal) and using a neutral color palette enhances an attic's airiness. Bringing in lightweight, small-scaled furnishings that best fit under the eaves also keeps it looking streamlined.

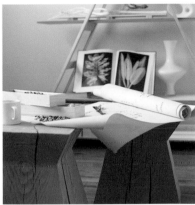

# Signature Style

Any room benefits from a creative approach to design. A home office is especially distinctive if it reflects your work's character.

Resourceful ideas are the foundation of one-of-a-kind style. Even if you're designing on a budget, there are plenty of ways to give any room a signature style if you adopt an inventive approach to furnishing.

Office furniture can be assembled from the most basic components. While store-bought modular pieces offer great flexibility, try inventing your own: create a desk by placing a sheet of wood over two filing cabinets or saw-horses; fashion a shelving unit from boards and storage cubes or planks and a stepladder. For inspiration, look to the work that you do. Gear decorative displays to a work theme, and make a virtue of necessity by showing off the tools of your trade and fruits of your labor.

## WHY THIS ROOM WORKS

A landscape designer grows a business in this serene, garden-like setting with its fresh color palette, inventive furnishings, and work-related decorative displays.

■ A SAWHORSE-BASE DESK topped with wood blends with the natural surroundings and is a low-cost way to create a large work surface.

■ SIMPLE WOODEN SHELVING UNITS are sturdy yet inexpensive.

■ A SOFT, BRIGHT WALL COLOR is an ideal backdrop for exotic plants and botanical artwork.

■ CLIENT PRESENTATIONS and work books contribute to the decor.

■ MODULAR WOOD STOOLS are reminiscent of tree trunks and bring the spirit of the outdoors inside.

■ ARMLESS UPHOLSTERED CHAIRS are easily rearranged to create a comfortable conference area.

■ WINDOW SHUTTERS block glare and offer privacy but let in sunlight.

# A Meeting Place

Part of good design is creating a space that suits all of its users. A polished workplace is a pleasure for you and your clients alike.

Inviting clients and associates into your office is one of the joys of working from home. You get the pleasure of welcoming guests into your personal space in a way that's just not possible in a corporate setting. To impart a professional impression, make sure the room offers the comforts of home but has a businesslike demeanor. This doesn't mean standard office furniture is required. Any furnishings that are clean-lined but comfortable can project an at-work ethic. Choose rugs, coffee tables, floor lamps, and accessories that add a casual sense of ease. Display colorful aspects of your character in the room to add personality and warmth. A bulletin-board collage or a favorite collection on the bookshelves gives visitors a peek into your personal life.

## WHY THIS ROOM WORKS

This light-filled attic room uses no traditional office furniture yet it has a professional feel. An eclectic blend of furnishings works together to create a homelike setting for business.

■ A MIX OF FURNITURE STYLES creates a more personal mood than a suite of matching office furniture: a contemporary chair is paired with midcentury lamps and a retooled vintage loveseat.

■ THE MOBILE DESK is an oak library table set on casters. It's positioned by the window to take advantage of natural light, but it can be moved against the wall to make space for larger meetings.

■ AN OVERHEAD SHELF, built between the eaves, holds flat files out of the sightlines of visitors.

■ A CHALKBOARD TABLE adds a touch of whimsy and lets callers jot down notes and numbers while using the phone.

■ THE SIMPLE PALETTE of white walls with brown and black furnishings projects a handsome, professional air.

With so many hours of our lives spent working, it's well worth the time and effort to create a workspace that is as beautiful as it is functional. And since it's an integral part of your home, there's every reason to make it as inviting and well-planned as your living room or bedroom. When determining the decor of your home office, look to your other rooms for clues on color and style. Especially if your office is within the traffic flow of the rest of the house, you'll need it to blend in with

# WORKING IN STYLE

A HOME OFFICE IS AT ITS BEST WHEN IT LETS YOUR PERSONALITY SHINE THROUGH. CREATE AN ENVIRONMENT THAT STIMULATES AND INSPIRES YOU TO DO YOUR BEST WORK.

the surroundings, so design it with a color palette, furnishings, and accessories that are consistent with the style of adjoining rooms. If your office shares a room used for other purposes, a cohesive style is even more important. All that said, if you're fortunate enough to have a separate space, indulge in a little luxury. You've made it to your own executive suite, so invest in well-crafted furnishings and fine finishes, and treat yourself to a terrific desk lamp or accent piece that you'll love looking at. Likewise, be imaginative with displays. You're free to reveal more of yourself than the standard family photo, so bring in artwork and personal collections.

# In Good
# Working Order

An office that's open to view demands a clear sense of order to maintain its style. Keep projects contained in neat walls of storage.

Order helps establish a sense of calm, and that becomes increasingly important when your home office is also used by the family for other purposes. Put miscellany in its place and you'll have a harmonious haven for all of a workroom's different functions.

One of the best ways to contain office hodgepodge is to take advantage of wall space. The smartest options for a neat look include modular storage and bookshelf arrangements. Shelving is extremely versatile and makes room for everything from reference books and neatly arranged baskets of paperwork to favorite objects or collections. Cabinets or bins with doors or lids conceal the odds and ends that might otherwise disorder a work surface. If you paint shelving or storage units the same color as the walls, the units will be less obtrusive and will have a built-in appearance.

## WHY THIS ROOM WORKS

With an abundance of desk space and modular wall storage, this office also functions as a family study and den. The symmetrical bookshelves and distinctively arranged cube cabinets bring orderliness to the room.

■ **WALL-MOUNTED FILE CABINETS** provide concealed storage and, arranged in a random pattern, work as an artistic display.

■ **BUILT-IN BOOKSHELVES** contain reference materials for work and books for family reading, honoring both functions of the space.

■ **THE TOP LEVEL OF SHELVING** is kept clear of objects and clutter, preserving a sense of spaciousness that would be sacrificed if it were filled.

■ **A WHITE COLOR SCHEME** creates an illusion of a larger room. The white work surface and storage units all appear to recede into the walls.

■ **A CONTEMPORARY SOFA** adds an energetic punch of color. Its sleek style is perfectly suited to the room's sense of order and openness.

An upper-level landing serves as a compact home office that takes advantage of outdoor views. Unique sliding bookshelves keep the space clutter-free and wide open.

■ AN L-SHAPED DESK tucks into the corner of the stair railing. Its glass top and slim construction preserve a feeling of expansive airiness.

■ A SLIDING WALL of shelves divides the office from an adjoining bedroom and pulls shut for bedroom privacy.

■ MAGNETIC CLIPBOARDS fit into the shelves and provide display space and a place for notes and memos in this room with few walls.

■ A PLUMP SOFA offers a comfortable spot for reading or meetings – or an afternoon catnap.

WORKING IN STYLE

# An Office Landing

In an open space, creating a harmony of style between your office and the rest of the house is an essential part of successful planning.

When choosing a spot for an office, you may not have a room to spare, but you might still have room. Pick an area in your home where there's at least a partial wall that you can devote to a bookshelf, and enough floor space for a desk and chair, and create your office there. A generous stair landing, hallway, alcove, porch, or bay window might suffice, with a little planning.

The most important aspect of making this work is creating a harmony of style. Furnish the office in ways that echo the surrounding or adjoining room's decor to maintain your home's cohesive look. For an in-the-open office, it's best to choose furnishings that occupy little visual space. Avoid heavy office furniture and opt instead for pieces with glass tops and slender profiles. Find ways, too, to ensure that you won't be disturbed during working hours. Creative design elements such as sliding doors, curtains, and screens close off space when necessary but maintain a sense of flow.

ADD STYLE AND WIT TO YOUR WORK
SPACE WITH VINTAGE ACCESSORIES.
CLEVERLY REPURPOSED TREASURES
BRING ORDER TO MAIL AND PAPERS.

An antique hotel mailbox, *opposite top*, is mounted on a wall and given new life as a bill sorter.

A metal letter "U," *opposite bottom*, part of an old shop sign, finds new purpose as a magnetic memo board. A combination of magnetized clips, pushpin-style magnets, and small dot magnets are used to make sure business cards, notes, and clippings are easy to find when you need them.

A gilded picture frame, *left*, with a glass inset, is put to work as a bulletin board. Notes and photos are taped to the surface, and a dry-erase marker writes easily on the glass.

Letter caddies, *above*, can be custom-made or cannily reinvented. A pair of springs are stretched between two U-bolts (top); a vintage toast rack becomes an organizer for oversized envelopes (bottom).

Sometimes the only way to find space for a home office is to press another room into service and create a dual-use space. Kitchens, bedrooms, guest rooms, and family rooms all can be recruited to offer at least part-time office area without sacrificing their original functions or atmospheres. When considering candidates for an office spot, think about how the space is generally used. If a room tends to lie dormant during the daytime, you can probably claim at least one of its walls for a primary

# WORKING
## IN A SHARED SPACE

DIFFERENT ROOMS OFFER DIFFERENT ADVANTAGES FOR A WORKSPACE, BUT WITH CAREFUL PLANNING, YOU CAN CREATE A SEAMLESS BLEND OF HOME AND OFFICE IN MOST ANY ROOM.

workspace. Also, base your decision on the type and amount of work you do. Kitchens are better suited to lighter tasks like paying bills and making schedules; bedroom offices are well suited to reading and writing but less welcoming to office equipment or piles of paperwork. A family room or infrequently used guest room, where you can carve out a larger area, usually works best if you're setting up a full-time home office. Wherever you site it, design and style your office in ways that keep it comfortable and residential; look for furniture, light fixtures, and accents that harmonize the overall space and extend a sense of home.

An all-white family room hosts a spacious office in a corner behind an ample sofa. The fabrics and color scheme are the same throughout the space, making the work area a natural extension of the living area.

■ A BUILT-IN SOFA functions as a half-wall and dividing partition. In a space-saving design, its frame incorporates a narrow work surface behind it.

■ OFFICE STORAGE is contained out of sight below the level of the sofa; open shelving puts some storage on display.

■ WALL-MOUNTED HALOGEN LIGHTS can be focused upward to fill the space with ambient lighting or downward for task or accent lighting. Desk lamps spotlight specific desk areas and add to an at-work feel.

WORKING IN A SHARED SPACE

# A Corner Office

Take advantage of today's sizable family rooms. There's plenty of space to set up for work while preserving an area to relax and play.

Many homes offer the comfort and spaciousness of a bonus or family room. These are ideal places to section off a home office since they're often free for use during the day when kids are at school or out at play.

To ensure that family time doesn't distract from work hours – and vice versa – you'll need to define some boundaries around the office area. Furniture placement and lighting can help here. Position a large piece of furniture like a sofa, bookcase, or entertainment center to form a "wall" behind which you'll work. In a casual family space like this, you don't want a complete barrier, just a subtle divider that delineates your work zone. You can use lighting to reinforce the line between living and work areas, too. Spotlights, wall fixtures, and desk or ceiling lights focused on the workspace let you "turn off" work when it's time to focus on family and friends. As with any divided space, maintain a cohesive decor across both areas to keep it attractive.

# A Bedroom Office

Bringing work into the bedroom can be a pleasure when your office space blends in serenely with the rest of the room.

It's challenging to bring a workspace into a room that's devoted to rest, but a thoughtful choice of furnishings can create harmony between sleeping and working areas. Planning a bedroom office carefully means you won't be interrupted by work when it's time to sleep, and the bed won't beckon when it's time to work.

Whatever your bedroom's decor, there's such a range of work surfaces and storage units available that you're bound to find one in a compatible style. You may also choose from a whole array of residential furniture that can effortlessly make a switch to office work, such as dining tables or consoles and upholstered chairs.

There are other tricks to blending a workspace into a bedroom. Choosing dual-purpose furniture – using a small desk as a nightstand or vanity, for example – keeps a space subdued. Decorative storage pieces also preserve the sense of serenity by stylishly containing clutter.

## WHY THIS ROOM WORKS

An entire workspace fits peacefully into an alcove of this bedroom. The architecture subtly defines the office, and the furnishings blend in effortlessly with the serene mood.

■ RESIDENTIAL FURNISHINGS at the desk – a table lamp and an upholstered chair on casters – fit well into a bedroom setting.

■ A DINING-SIZE TABLE suits the spacious bay and adds to the residential feel; its simple styling creates a tranquil, subdued effect.

■ A WOODEN BENCH, accessible from both areas, acts as an unobtrusive divider between work and sleep areas.

■ STACKS OF BOOKS topped by stones make attractive displays. They subtly reinforce the room's division.

Adds Up to a Championship Game

Feeling No Pressure,
The Illini Smile Again

RELAXING

"MY DREAM HOME INCLUDES PLACES FOR PURE RELAXATION. I WANT EVERY SPACE TO OFFER REASONS TO STOP AND LINGER, TO MAKE RELAXING IRRESISTIBLE."

# LEISURE SPACE

Everyone needs down time, and if you make room for relaxation in your life, you're actually more likely to take the opportunity to unwind. All throughout your home, indoors and out, find ways to carve out spaces that are so soothing and inviting that you simply have to slow down and settle in.

Leisure time means different things to different people and embraces every kind of activity, both solitary and shared. So make the TV viewing area, the patio, your crafts room, the porch, and the kids' playroom all as enticing as you would your living room or bedroom. In the following pages, we'll show you easy ways to do this, to bring style and comfort to all the places where you and your family relax.

# How to Plan a Leisure Space

The best way to manage stress is to build free time into your schedule because, left to chance, you almost never take it. A similar rule applies to your home. Create spaces devoted to leisure, and your family will use them.

Communal activities have different requirements from solitary pursuits, but both deserve priority when decorating your house. At home you have the best opportunity to encourage children's talents and interests. One way to do that is to make sure there's room to pursue them. Making space for creativity is one tangible way to stress its significance. Space to work on your own projects is equally important. Look for an underused room – or just a portion of a room or even a large closet – that will allow you to enjoy your creative time without having to organize everything each time you want to work, whether on quilting or calligraphy, scrapbooking or woodcarving.

Setting up a media center is a popular way to bring the whole family together. Now often built right into new homes, media centers are also easily added to spaces within your current home. Basements and unused attics are well suited to movie watching because there are fewer windows to create glare on the screen. If you have a spare bedroom, that's another smart location because it's possible to darken the space with black-out shades or draperies with black-out linings. Closets are ready-made storage areas for overflow CDs, the DVD player, the receiver, and the satellite box. On the opposite page, we've outlined a number of things to keep in mind to ensure your enjoyment of a media center.

## A COMPACT MEDIA ROOM

A media room (above and preceding page) occupies a wide landing at the top of the second-floor stairs. Windows were excluded from this area to prevent glare on the screen.

■ SECTIONAL SEATING suits movie viewers of all ages. An ottoman on casters serves as a legrest or coffee table, or provides additional seating.

■ BLACK CABINETRY is a good choice surrounding a video screen. It makes the TV less noticeable when it's off and minimizes the visibility of speakers in the unit.

■ PLENTIFUL STORAGE is critical to contain all the paraphernalia associated with TV, movies, and music. Plan appropriately sized, built-in units to store similar items together, so that everything will be orderly.

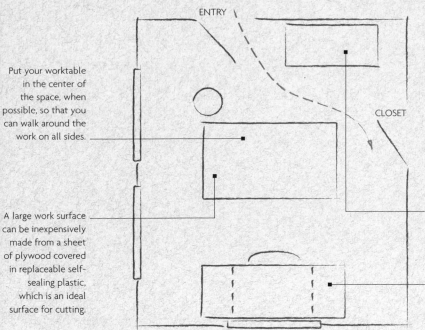

Put your worktable in the center of the space, when possible, so that you can walk around the work on all sides.

ENTRY

CLOSET

A large work surface can be inexpensively made from a sheet of plywood covered in replaceable self-sealing plastic, which is an ideal surface for cutting.

## A SEWING/CRAFTS ROOM

For anyone who passionately pursues an avocation, setting up a dedicated studio or workroom at home can be a turning point in nurturing the creative process. Even a space of your own needs a logical layout, however, so tailor it for your particular craft.

A shelving unit provides vertical storage without taking much floor space. Fill it with baskets that hold various materials.

Use file cabinets, stacked drawer units, and other storage systems as supports for a desk or worktable to make the most of available space.

## MEDIA CENTER CHECKLIST

A media center may be as deluxe as a room with tiered seating or as simple as modular pieces arranged to set up a viewing area.

### Seating Placement

Consider the amount of space you have available before racing out to buy an extra-large video screen. Viewing quality is influenced as much by distance from the screen as it is by screen size. To calculate the correct distance for seating, multiply the diagonal size of the screen by 2–2.5 for HDTV and by 4 for analog. For example, if your HDTV screen is 30" across (76 cm), the best viewing range is 60–75" (1.5–1.9 m) from the screen. A 57" (145 cm) screen is best viewed from a distance of 10–12' (3–3.5 m).

30" (76 cm)

60–75" (1.5–1.9 m)

### Cabinet

Most media center cabinets accept a wide range of screen sizes, but be sure to compare both the width and the depth of a cabinet with your TV's size.

### Speakers

For a multispeaker home theater setup, follow the manufacturer's guidelines for placement. In general, position left and right front speakers well apart and away from side walls, making sure the distance from you to each speaker is greater than the distance between the two speakers.

### Seating

Sectional sofa units seat a crowd comfortably and efficiently, but also consider including chairs on casters or other lightweight occasional chairs in your plan, for supplemental seating.

### Insulation

This is one room where rugs or wall-to-wall carpet and draperies are essential because hard surfaces distort sound.

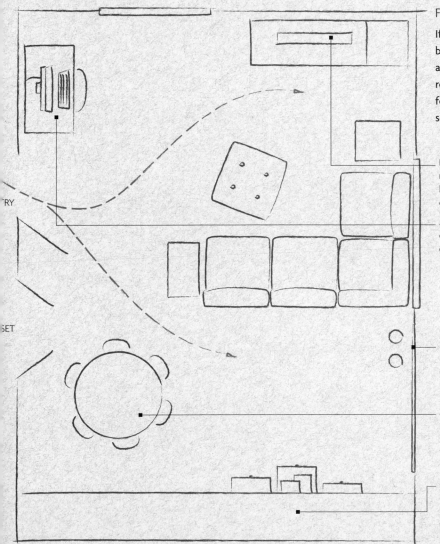

## FAMILY PLAYROOM

If you're lucky enough to have a bonus room in your home, make it a space where everyone wants to relax. This space is designed to work for everyone from toddlers to high school students and Mom and Dad.

Even a large screen works well on a modular TV stand. A companion cabinet holds stereo and other audio-video equipment and CDs and DVDs.

Adults can work at the family computer while keeping an eye on play activities.

A chalkboard wall is irresistible fun, and chalkboard paint can be applied directly to drywall. Store chalk and washable erasers in buckets nearby.

A play table needs to be low enough for children but large enough for their projects. Make sure it has a surface that can be wiped clean.

Utilize awkward space beneath a low attic ceiling by filling it with valuable storage areas. For smaller children, open cubbies keep toys accessible and easy to put away.

Media has changed almost beyond imagination in the last thirty years, and the way we live with it has changed, too. Concert-quality music piped throughout the house, on-demand movies appearing on flat screens, libraries of CDs and DVDs to choose from as the mood strikes – these pleasures have not only transformed the way we spend leisure time, they've also revolutionized the way that we organize our homes. Whether you have a separate room devoted to video entertainment or

# MAKING ROOM
# FOR MEDIA

THE BEST MEDIA STORAGE KEEPS EVERYTHING IN ORDER, MAKES THINGS EASY TO FIND IN AN INSTANT, AND FUNCTIONS AS A DECORATIVE ELEMENT IN ITS OWN RIGHT.

a large media center that shares another room of the house, order is a must if you want these spaces to be seamlessly integrated into your home. Fortunately, specially designed furniture is now made for housing electronic equipment, and it's available in styles that complement the decor of almost any room. Most pieces include room for accessories, with spaces for video or game hardware and drawers for remote controls. It also can be fun to find antique pieces and decorative containers in which to store media equipment and accessories. With all the options currently available, it's easy to make media storage both smart and stylish.

# Intuitive Storage

In a room dedicated to home entertainment,
a logical plan puts everything in its place and
keeps the space uncluttered and attractive.

Today's families have continually growing collections of
media but limited space in which to keep them. The
best way to maximize space and maintain order is with
customized storage. As with storage in any room, the
rule is to make it obvious and to keep it simple. Desig-
nating specific places for each kind of item you use
makes organization intuitive. Keep most-used things
in view and close at hand and the rest tucked away in
closed storage – kids' favorite DVDs in a bin near the
player, for example, and the remainder hidden in a cabinet or closet. Adjust the heights of shelves to plainly
signal what goes where, so that putting things back
where they belong requires little effort.

## WHY THIS ROOM WORKS

A smart storage system creates
a sense of order that lets everyone
who uses this media room know
exactly where everything belongs.

■ ADJUSTABLE SHELVING transforms
a closet into a storage cabinet for
electronic components, discs, tapes,
and photo albums. Shelves are tightly
positioned and adjusted for specific
contents, allowing maximum storage.

■ IDENTICAL BINDERS holding family
photographs, letters, and clippings
appear more orderly because of their
matching size and color.

■ CLEAR PLASTIC BINS for CDs keep
current favorites close at hand, so you
don't have to flip through your entire
collection to find them.

■ OPEN SHELVING is reserved for
frequently used items that can be
attractively stored.

■ A REMOTE CONTROL CADDY kept
in plain sight is the surest way to find
controls when they're needed.

pop hits

lounge

classical

This sophisticated family room plays down its role as media central, so it's as inviting for reading or game playing as it is for TV viewing.

■ **CUBE-SHAPED SHELVING UNITS** make each display shelf a separate vignette within the larger grid, giving the wall an identity apart from its media function.

■ **A MEDIA CABINET** built into the center of the display wall is self-contained, with storage drawers stacked for easy access. Doors hide everything when the TV's not in use.

■ **EASY CHAIRS** are upholstered in washable suede, and ottomans in dark leather; both are easy-care options.

■ **A SOFT COLOR PALETTE** allows the display wall to take center stage.

MAKING ROOM FOR MEDIA

# A Balanced Display

A handsome display wall with customized storage cabinets puts media equipment in context, surrounding it with objects and art.

Building a media cabinet into the middle of a display wall is an effective and stylish storage solution. By surrounding a television screen with a grid of shelving, equal weight is given to your other interests and pastimes, and the display remains engaging with cabinet doors open or closed. This is an especially good idea for spaces that do double-duty such as family rooms, bedrooms, and studies. Media accessories and related equipment should be stored as close to the TV as possible, so plan for extra drawers and shelves within the TV enclosure. Doors designed to slide back into the cabinet when open are also a clever idea.

For a media space that's shared with children, choose upholstery materials that are easily cleaned. Today, that includes leathers and washable suedes, so even family spaces can be furnished with sophisticated style. Cotton remains an easy-care option for upholstery, especially lightly textured chenilles and brushed twills.

Everyone has creative impulses of some kind, and having a special space in which to pursue them can be a life-changing luxury. Whether yours is a quiet art that requires little more than a pen and paper or one involving a shop, a lathe, or a potter's wheel, having a place to pursue the task that you love is important for maintaining a balance in life. It might be as small as a desk in the corner of the kitchen or as grand as an attic atelier. The important thing is, it's all yours. The best

# INSPIRING
# CREATIVITY

THE SPACE WHERE YOU PURSUE YOUR HOBBIES AND PASSIONS SHOULD BE PERSONALLY INSPIRING. PLAN IT WITH CARE, FURNISH IT WITH COMFORT, AND INFUSE IT WITH CHARACTER.

creative spaces are a mix: half organization, half inspiration. Begin by carving out an area that's suited to the demands of your projects. Create a sense of order with well-planned furnishings, lighting, and storage, setting things up in ways that reflect the process of your craft. Then focus on the details. To ensure creating work that you're proud of, surround yourself with objects that you love and that inspire you, and provide plenty of shelf space for reference books and magazines. As much as possible, establish a sense of privacy, and bring in an easy chair and other amenities that encourage you to take time out for contemplation.

# A Sunlit Studio

Artists seek the purity of unfiltered daylight to practice their craft. The best creative spaces celebrate natural light and honor order.

Visual artists need – and in fact insist upon – lots of natural sunlight. Applying this preference to your own space will help to keep you energized and inspired, regardless of the project at hand.

Whether your creative space holds an easel, a writing desk, a woodworking bench, or a crafting table, keep things simply organized. Position work surfaces to take advantage of the greatest amount of daylight; northern light is ideal, but natural light of any kind tends to stimulate creativity and improve mood. To enjoy maximum sunlight from your windows, choose sheer drapes or shades – or, if privacy allows, take full advantage of the room's light by opting for bare windows instead.

## WHY THIS ROOM WORKS

Flooded with light and furnished with restraint, this calligrapher's studio gives everyday tools and works-in-progress pride of place.

■ UNSHADED WINDOWS on two sides of the room bathe the artist's desk in natural light.

■ A WOODEN SECRETARY, whose small scale fits this room, provides storage space for finished drawings and art supplies and affords display space for favorite books and objects.

■ SAMPLES OF WORK, suspended from ordinary twine, catch the light and become decorative elements in their own right.

■ STACKED BOOKS on the floor contribute an offhand air and a touch of color and leave walls unadorned.

■ AN ADJUSTABLE WORK LIGHT clips to the drafting table to supplement natural or overhead ambient light at night or on cloudy days.

# Organic Design

A rustic but orderly garden potting shed offers valuable lessons about organization that are applicable to every kind of creative space.

"Everything in its place" is more than just an obvious catchphrase. It's a philosophy that any creative person can benefit from. Every activity has its own natural order, so pay attention to the rhythms of your work, and set up your space accordingly.

A well-organized potting shed is a perfect example. It allocates different areas for specific chores — starting seedlings, repotting plants, studying horticulture manuals or magazines — and includes carefully planned storage for all necessities: stakes, soil, fertilizer, seeds, and so on. There's a place to store tools and a place to clean them, and there's even room for valued mementos and collections, to give the space a personal touch.

## WHY THIS ROOM WORKS

A weathered backyard potting shed, outfitted with shelves, buckets, and galvanized counters, provides a pleasant and efficient spot to spend the day gardening or organizing.

■ MULTIPLE WORK AREAS are organized as you would a kitchen. Wet areas, where soil spills over from repotting, are separated from dry sections for drawing plans or reading.

■ A GALVANIZED TUB filled with dry sand cleans hand tools with a swipe, then stores them, preventing rust.

■ WOODEN DRAWERS are partitioned to separate small ties, labels, and seed packets, which could get mislaid without an organizing system.

■ SALVAGED MATERIALS are well suited to a rough-and-ready garden shed. With a coat of white paint, they all work together visually.

■ A COLLECTION OF PADLOCKS adds wit and personality to the space.

WHY THIS ROOM WORKS

## WHY THIS ROOM WORKS

In a painter's studio, a confident use of color, clever displays of tools and supplies, and an intelligent use of space creates a workplace that's as appealing as a gallery.

■ **A PLEXIGLAS SHEET**, supported a few inches above the desktop by plumbing brackets, creates a handsome display case for smaller tools and supplies.

■ **OPEN STORAGE UNITS**, pushed together to form a central worktable, allow free flow of traffic and access to storage from all sides.

■ **MULTIPLE STORAGE CONTAINERS** are as clever as they are attractive. Cans, jars, shelves, boxes, totes — even a carpenter's tool caddy — all limit clutter and contribute visual order.

INSPIRING CREATIVITY

# A Painter's Eye

When setting up a studio, think like an artist. An imaginative approach to storage and space planning infuses a room with personality.

Artists are adept at finding order in chaos, and that's a talent that sometimes extends to their surroundings as well as their work. The imaginative eye of an artist turned to the physical setup of a studio results in a room that's as distinctive as an artwork.

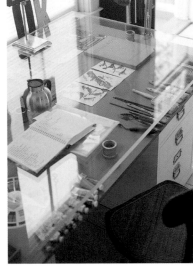

Finding creative and witty ways to store tools, materials, and works-in-progress brings visual harmony to a space and adds touches of whimsy. Look for inspired ideas for repurposing unusual containers — mounting paint cans on a wall for "in" and "out" boxes, for example — or interesting ways to reimagine storage, like using a child's chair to hold frequently used materials. Think creatively about space, consolidating storage in ways that make the most of the room you have. Organizing storage along walls gives you room to move freely in the center of the space; focusing storage in a central workstation allows access from all sides and creates aisles for passage around it.

You don't need a trip to the woods or the seashore to gain the benefits of being outdoors. It's never been easier to enjoy the open air. Simply look to your own backyard. Whatever size yard or patio you have, make the best use of it by creating a space that invites you to get outside and relax. Outdoor areas are often the last to get decorating attention, but they shouldn't be. Make them as comfortable as the rest of your home, carrying your sense of style through to outdoor furnishings,

# ENJOYING THE
# OPEN AIR

THE NATURAL RESPONSE TO FINE WEATHER IS TO GET OUT AND ENJOY IT. MAKE THE MOST OF THE SEASON BY CUSTOMIZING OUTDOOR SPACES FOR CAREFREE RELAXATION.

whether country casual, ocean-liner chic, or cabana cool. Fashionable weather-resistant fabrics allow you to coordinate accessories just as you would in your living room. What are your favorite open-air pleasures? Plan spaces that make it easy for you to pursue the activity – or inactivity – that you love. Look for ways to add comfort: seating arranged for easy conversation, ample table surfaces for drinks and food, and plump cushions that encourage lounging. Finishing touches like linens, candles, lanterns, and accessories give an outdoor space your personal stamp, while extra towels, throws, and pillows make guests feel right at home.

# Cabana Style

Thoughtfully furnished, a poolside cabana can become everyone's favorite room throughout the entire warm-weather season.

The key to relaxed outdoor living is combining beauty and comfort with the benefits of easy care. That means providing welcoming seating and gracious amenities for everyone, but making sure that furnishings can weather heavy use. Choose practical furniture crafted from hardwoods that stand up to the elements. Supply plenty of pillows and cushions in bright colors that celebrate the outdoors; choose washable or weather-friendly fabrics to ensure that they'll stay fresh-looking all season long. Create inviting places to escape the sun with weather-resistant canvas patio umbrellas or awnings. Stock up on durable tableware, and add thoughtful touches like rolled towels and water bottles.

## WHY THIS ROOM WORKS

Designed around two separate areas, this poolside setup offers an irresistible invitation for guests to enjoy themselves in the sun or to gather and relax in the shade.

■ WEATHER-RESISTANT LOUNGERS, fitted with terry cloth–slipcovered cushions in bright colors, are equipped with built-in beverage trays. A milkman's basket filled with flip-flops invites guests to help themselves.

■ CANVAS MARKET UMBRELLAS near the pool provide protection when bathers are ready for some shade. A poolside pavilion with canvas curtains and comfortable seating offers a place to gather and snack out of the sun.

■ TEAK BENCHES double as cocktail tables and can be moved outdoors as needed for parties.

■ COLORFUL PLASTIC TRAYS are a practical choice for a poolside setting. Frozen lemon and lime slices are tasty alternatives to ice cubes.

# An Urban Escape

A small balcony garden can be every bit as relaxing as a large yard. Create a piece of paradise in even the tiniest of outdoor spots.

City dwellers need as much open-air relaxation as their country counterparts. Luckily, it's fairly simple to create a serene green space on a patio or balcony. First, look at scale. The furniture and plant containers you choose should be appropriately sized for the setting. A few well-chosen smaller-sized pieces can give the impression of a fully furnished space, and even a single row of leafy perennials can provide a sense of enclosure. Next, choose durable, lightweight materials; plastic containers on casters make it easy to rotate plants as needed to give each its time in the sun. Finally, don't forget lighting; several solar-powered lights staked in the planters add drama and give a garden a finished look at night.

## WHY THIS ROOM WORKS

This small city balcony has the impact of a larger garden, thanks to its smart sense of proportion. Plants and furnishings fill the space without overwhelming it.

■ LUSH PLANTINGS arranged in lightweight plastic pots soften the balcony's edges and create the look of a border garden.

■ WEATHERED PLANKS add to the natural look of the balcony; they can be laid on top of concrete to give a city patio a more rustic look.

■ SOLAR-POWERED lanterns and orbs cast a soft glow by night. Requiring only six hours of sunlight to recharge, solar lights are as environmentally wise as they are aesthetically pleasing.

■ A POWDER-COATED METAL TABLE is weather resistant and scaled for a small space. A seagrass slipper chair, moved outdoors in good weather, provides a soft spot to relax. Seagrass pieces used inside the house give a room a relaxed feel.

## WHY THIS ROOM WORKS

The charms of this boathouse are enhanced by low-maintenance, high-comfort furnishings and personal accents that play off a nautical theme.

■ **A PALE WASH OF PAINT** on the simple plywood walls unifies the space and makes it seem larger; it's also a good foil for brighter accents.

■ **PEGBOARD PANELS** define a walk-in closet for storing boating and water-sports equipment, and provide extra room for family members' belongings.

■ **FAMILY PHOTOS AND MEMORABILIA** give the space the personality and style of an indoor room.

■ **BOATING HOOKS** double as towel and tackle hooks and even make handles for an improvised serving tray.

ENJOYING THE OPEN AIR

# A Boathouse Family Room

Furnished with the comforts of an indoor room, an open-air boathouse is a perfect retreat for a family that lives at water's edge.

When there's nowhere you'd rather be than on the water, why go back to the house to relax after you've docked the boat? Turn the protected space of a boathouse into a family room and extend afternoons on the water into evenings at its edge. All you need are a few comfortable places to stretch out — sectional pieces are wonderfully adaptable — and some personal touches that connect the space to home and family.

Let the bright colors and distinctive shapes of the boating gear inform the decor. Choose lightweight furnishings that are easily moved to storage or back to the house at season's end, and use tough, mildew-resistant fabric for seat coverings. Create a spot to stow equipment like skis and fishing rods, but don't make a fuss about hiding it all from view; the most important views here are the ones looking out to nature.

# A Shady Grove

A tree-shaded haven for garden parties, get-togethers, and lawn games is a refined but easy addition to a spacious backyard.

If you've ever admired those big luncheon parties so often seen in foreign films, set in outdoor groves and accompanied by games of bocce ball, you're not alone. The good news is, that's an atmosphere that can be reproduced in your own backyard. Fast-growing trees planted in rows quickly create an outdoor "room" that can be enjoyed for generations to come.

As a landscaping upgrade, this is one of the easiest designs to start from scratch, and one of the most dramatic. Choose a spot, and plant equal-length rows of fast-growers like poplars, willows, or aspens. A simple crushed gravel surface, well suited to shade, games, and foot traffic, completes the design.

## WHY THIS ROOM WORKS

Finishing touches turn this essentially simple setting into a picture-perfect location for family reunions and long afternoons at the table or on the game court.

■ A CRISP LINEN TABLECLOTH and plump cushions on the wooden benches contribute to the festive atmosphere. They make even a rustic picnic table look luxurious.

■ CERAMIC PLATES instead of paper, and proper cutlery instead of plastic, are small amenities that make guests feel genuinely indulged.

■ EXTRA CHAIRS, arranged in pairs and groups, encourage intimate conversations or can be pulled up to the ends of the table.

■ HURRICANE LAMPS set firmly in gravel, and lights strung from overhead branches cast a magical spell over evenings outdoors.

■ STRAW HATS are tongue-in-cheek accessories for an afternoon of old-fashioned fun and games.

NAPPING IN THE SHADE IS PURE WARM-WEATHER BLISS. PICK YOUR SPOT AND SET UP A COZY RETREAT FOR AN AFTERNOON SNOOZE.

**An all-weather chaise**, *above left*, is a welcome sight for swimmers ready for some rest and relaxation. Position it beneath an overhang or patio umbrella and dress it with waterproof cushions, pillows, and a light blanket to ward off a chill.

**A canvas tent pavilion**, *left*, is its own outdoor room. To make it comfortable for the entire summer, furnish it with amenities like a folding camp bed, a portable stove, and plenty of pillows.

**A lightweight portable cot**, *above*, makes setting up a backyard sleeping station a two-minute affair. All you have to do is grab your folding lounger and a pillow and blanket, and head for the nearest shady spot.

**A classic hammock**, *right*, is a summertime staple that's hard to resist. At the beginning of the season, string one up between a pair of shade trees or on a covered porch, and you'll have a perfect spot for napping in the breeze.

COLOR

"COLOR HAS THE POWER TO CALM, COMFORT, ENERGIZE, AND INSPIRE. I WANT TO BRING COLOR TO EVERY ROOM OF MY HOME AND HAVE IT WORK TOGETHER BEAUTIFULLY."

# Choosing Color

If you're looking for a color change, begin by identifying a range of hues that you respond to. Within our palettes you'll find a plan for harmonizing color throughout your home.

One of the most common questions Pottery Barn receives from customers is what paint color was used in one of the rooms in our catalog. We address that question by presenting our favorite wall colors and explaining the reasons we choose them. Our color choices are divided into two broad categories, neutral and earthy colors, and saturated and soft ones. Within each category, the palettes we favor tend to be muted: more dusty than bright, warm but not hot, comfortable rather than dramatic. These are colors

that speak with resonance but never shout, reflecting our philosophy that the colors you choose should enhance, not overpower, the furnishings in a room.

Even if you're only painting one room, it's helpful to begin by mapping out a color plan for the entire house. You'll find that creating a soothing flow of colors from room to room establishes a unified environment in your home and simplifies the process of choosing colors for each space. Use the examples on the opposite page as a starting point. Note that with all color swatches shown in this book, we've listed the name and reference number of the closest Benjamin Moore paint color. Because color printing processes can alter the way color appears, be sure to test swatches of any color that you are considering.

## LIGHT AND VALUE

A hue may have a whole range of tones that skew lighter or darker, and appears to change in different lighting.

■ NATURAL LIGHT AND SHADOW transform the appearance of a paint color into graduated values of the original, as seen above; they almost appear to be different colors. Make sure you test a color in both daylight and artificial light to see its range.

■ VALUE denotes the lightness or darkness of a hue. Above, lighter values (tints) of the wall color appear at the top of the row of brushstrokes, and move to darker values (shades) at the bottom. Choosing different values of one color that you love is an effective way to coordinate colors from room to room.

## BUILDING A COLOR PLAN

Planning color for the entire house makes a more cohesive statement because each color is supported by others in a harmonious palette.

■ HUES OF THE SAME VALUE are used to help unify different wall colors that will be seen together, such as the living room, library, and entry hall.

■ IN THE ENTRY HALL, choose a color that makes a smooth transition, to harmonize with adjoining rooms.

■ THE LIBRARY'S WARM TAUPE calls for a complementary lighter gray in the kitchen and breakfast area.

■ THE PORCH has walls painted the same color as the adjacent kitchen. To further connect the spaces, the blue-green of the kitchen cabinets is repeated on the ceiling of the porch.

■ THE DINING ROOM stays within warm neutrals but skews more tan than gray.

■ THE TRIM is painted throughout with Simply White, a slightly warm white.

Simply White 2143-70

Clay Beige OC-11

Collingwood OC-28

Cape Hatteras Sand AC-34

Horizon Gray 2141-50

Buxton Blue HC-149

Winter Gates AC-30

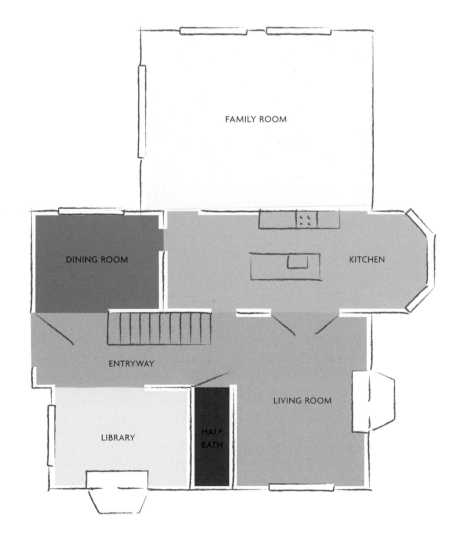

## COLOR IN AN OPEN PLAN

When several different rooms or spaces are seen together, it's especially important to coordinate a palette for the entire house.

■ START WITH ONE COLOR that you love. For example, this plan begins with the deep rust color used in the dining room. A lighter hue is used in the library across the hall, to temper the dining room's dramatic color.

■ SATURATED COLORS like Gold Rush and the darker brown used in the half bath are often better reserved for areas that are used occasionally rather than seen every day.

■ CONTINUE THE ENTRYWAY COLOR into the living room, as a directional clue. Here a medium-range taupe complements adjoining rooms.

■ CHOOSE A NEUTRAL COLOR for a central space and build upon it. A light stone color anchors the kitchen, the taupe gives the living room a little more weight, and the cream used in the family room plays up its spaciousness.

■ TRIM COLOR is Super White, a very pure white that affords a crisp look.

Super White

Elephant Tusk OC-8

Philadelphia Cream HC-30

Hot Spring Stones AC-31

Shenandoah Taupe AC-36

Gold Rush 2166-10

Middlebury Brown HC-68

Neutral and earthy colors are hues based in nature that evoke a grounded sense of well-being – stone, cream, sky, jade, terra-cotta, and mustard are all good examples. Our favorite neutral colors are found at the lighter end of this group, our earthy hues at the darker end (see the individual palettes on the following pages). Neutral colors bring a sense of tranquility to a room, and they're also a great base upon which you can layer more intense colors. Adding touches of warmer hues gives depth to a

# NEUTRAL
## AND EARTHY COLORS

AGREEABLE AND EASY TO LIVE WITH, THESE TONES ARE THE MOST VERSATILE COLOR CHOICES. FOR A NATURALLY SOOTHING HOME, TAKE ADVANTAGE OF THEIR RELAXING EFFECT.

room; in general, warm neutrals like creams and tans pair well with red and yellow accents. Cooler neutrals like grays and whites are best accented with crisp blues and hues from the cooler end of the palette. Earthy colors are a natural extension of neutrals but tend to be richer and warmer. Their intensity can be played up or down to suit your taste and the amount of light in a room. Use a stronger earthy color on just a single wall, for instance, if you want a quieter effect or if the room tends to be dark. Add some spark to deep earthy hues with clear, sharp colors such as chartreuse or sunny yellow to bring a contemporary attitude to a space.

# Selecting a Neutral Color Palette

In the world of color, neutral does not mean bland. Neutrals encompass a whole range of subtle variations and have hints of blue, green, red, or yellow. A room is given elegance and depth by layering closely related hues.

Neutrals are the chameleons of the color world, an almost infinite range of whites, grays, and tans that can run warm or cool and that change in response to subtle changes in light throughout the day. Depending upon a neutral's color value – how light or dark its shade is – it can serve as either a dominant or a background color. Used together in a variety of values, neutrals add quiet texture. Because they carry the flow between rooms with more subtlety than any other palette, they are a natural choice for open-plan houses.

Neutral paint colors all have a base that includes red, yellow, green, or blue; this undertone will be more apparent when the paint is on your walls. For instance, a true tan has a hint of red in it, khaki leans toward green, and another tan may have yellow highlights. Similarly, gray skews warmer or cooler depending on how much red or blue is in its base. While it's hard to discern the difference when looking at a single color, it's easy to see when you put several neutrals together.

When choosing colors, be sure to consider the tones of wooden floors, built-in cabinets, carpeting, and fixed architectural features such as stone or brickwork in the surrounding space – oak, for example, is enhanced by warmer tones. Choose a wall color that harmonizes with the undertones of the room's materials, or select a contrasting hue to highlight their colors.

## A NEUTRAL MOOD BOARD

Gathering samples of colors and objects that appeal to you and creating a "mood board" is a good place to start when choosing color.

■ A MUTED PALETTE requires an especially lively mix of textures to enhance the room's visual interest. Incorporate velvets, linens, and other textural weaves for variety.

■ LOOK FOR NATURAL ELEMENTS like rocks, shells, straw, or distressed wood; rougher textures enhance an informal attitude in a neutral space.

■ CREATE CONTRAST by juxtaposing warm with cool. You don't need bright colors to add variety – use a pale lavender-blue to contrast with a warm gray or tan, for example.

Simply White 2143-70

Super White

Snow White 2122-70

Calm OC-22

Vanilla Ice Cream 2154-70

Misty Gray 2124-60

Vanilla Milkshake 2141-70

Lily White 2128-70

Collingwood OC-28

Elephant Tusk OC-8

American White 2112-70

Gray Owl OC-52

Bunny Gray 2124-50

Hot Spring Stones AC-31

Monroe Bisque HC-26

Cement Gray 2112-60

Horizon Gray 2141-50

Beacon Gray 2128-60

Cape Hatteras Sand AC-34

Clay Beige OC-11

Stormy Monday 2112-50

Sea Haze 2137-50

November Skies 2128-50

Quincy Tan HC-25

Winter Gates AC-30

Boothbay Gray HC-165

Deep Silver 2124-30

### Perfectly White, *left*

Whites are the ultimate neutrals. Here a creamy white wall color is matched with a range of warm white hues in furnishings and accessories and complemented with accent pieces like burnished wood and supple leather. Though the room is predominantly monochromatic, it reads as warm and welcoming, thanks to a careful balance of highlights and undertones.

### Paired Colors, *right*

A warmer tan wall in a bedroom is well matched with a pale yellow in the adjoining hallway, which picks up its undertones. When planning color, be sure to consider the view from one room to the next. The golden tones of the wood flooring and the intriguing bedside table also harmonize well with the paint colors. Paint on the mouldings and cabinetry is a rich white that, along with the white silk and cotton bedding, provides a crisp counterpoint to the warm scheme.

### Handsome Understatement, *left*

Warm gray is anything but drab when it's used in a sophisticated mix. Paired with deep brown wood cabinetry, stone countertops, and neat white trim and window treatments, this bathroom's wall color is subdued and calming — just what's called for in a room designed for restoration and relaxation. The space's sleekness is nicely balanced with a rich range of textures: a terry cloth cover on the window seat, stacks of towels, a braided rug, and a display of sponges.

# Selecting an Earthy Color Palette

Introducing the organic colors of the earth into your home is a simple way to ground it in a sense of natural warmth. The deep, beautiful hues of nature are timeless and are consistently a pleasure to live with.

Earthy colors are those found in nature: charcoal, chestnut, ochre, persimmon, plum, terra-cotta. They are elemental, familiar, and reassuring. Though our selected earth tones tend to be darker than neutrals and make more of a visual statement, they have a similar muted quality. We especially like these hues because of the sense of comfort they bring to a room, and also for their versatility: earth tones are neither masculine nor feminine. Although these colors naturally complement rustic or informal rooms, they also lend themselves to more refined living rooms, forming a perfect backdrop for jewel-toned upholstery. Earth tones are a good choice in rooms that feature natural materials such as wooden beams or flooring, or stone or brick fireplaces. They are also well suited to spaces that see everyday use like family rooms or bedrooms, where the snug, cocooning effect of deeper shades is especially welcome. In a media room, using a darker earthtone cuts glare and makes onscreen colors appear brighter.

Despite earth tones' richness, they work well with a wide variety of accent colors. They look sophisticated, crisp, and tailored when paired with a creamy white trim; for a layered, more organic feel, use a more muted shade of the main room color or another earthy hue for mouldings or accents.

## EARTHY INSPIRATIONS

When gathering samples for an earthy palette, remember to explore a wide range of hues – don't limit yourself to browns and terra-cotta.

- ■ **LOOK TO NATURE** for inspiration: even an earthy landscape often contains vibrant splashes of bolder color. Mix some stronger colors into your palette.

- ■ **KEEP TEXTURE IN MIND** when selecting color. The same hue in buttery leather evokes a different feeling in linen or chenille, where texture warms the hue.

- ■ **REMEMBER PATTERN:** Whether seen in the grid of a solid-colored basketweave or in the repeated motifs of a printed pattern fabric, pattern is a powerful element in any color scheme.

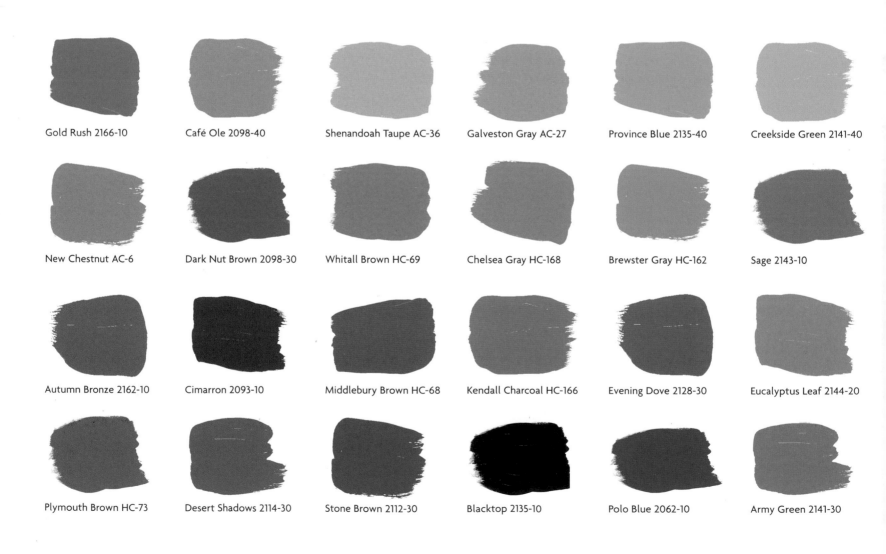

Gold Rush 2166-10  
Café Ole 2098-40  
Shenandoah Taupe AC-36  
Galveston Gray AC-27  
Province Blue 2135-40  
Creekside Green 2141-40  

New Chestnut AC-6  
Dark Nut Brown 2098-30  
Whitall Brown HC-69  
Chelsea Gray HC-168  
Brewster Gray HC-162  
Sage 2143-10  

Autumn Bronze 2162-10  
Cimarron 2093-10  
Middlebury Brown HC-68  
Kendall Charcoal HC-166  
Evening Dove 2128-30  
Eucalyptus Leaf 2144-20  

Plymouth Brown HC-73  
Desert Shadows 2114-30  
Stone Brown 2112-30  
Blacktop 2135-10  
Polo Blue 2062-10  
Army Green 2141-30

### Strong and Grounded, *left*

Earth tones are frequently thought of as tending toward browns and reds, but blues and greens are also drawn from nature, and are vital parts of an earthy palette. Here, a deep grayed-blue is a cooling complement to the red tones of the wood, and is picked up in the kilim-design pillows and rugs. The relatively dark value of the wall color is perfect for creating a soothing and sheltering atmosphere in this reading nook, which is part of a large open-plan space.

### Calm and Collected, *right*

This handsome study is appealingly lively yet subdued, due to its thoughtful balance of color. A tan on the walls, accented with fresh white trim and tailored Roman shades, gives the room a spacious feel. In contrast, deeper tones predominate on the floor and in the furnishings, creating a dynamic play between the lighter walls and the darker central areas: the deep browns and earth tones ground the space while the tan-and-white walls lift and expand it.

### Naturally Sophisticated, *right*

An earthy palette gives a sophisticated space natural appeal. Creamy coffee walls in a smart and casual living room look elegant with fresh white trim. Natural materials and accent pieces bring in complementary earth tones and add layers of texture – chenille, suede, leather, wood, and matchstick blinds at the windows. A burst of red on the sofa punctuates the palette and enlivens the color scheme.

Some people believe that no room is truly complete without a dash of red. If you're looking for a color that makes a statement, red is pretty much the front-runner, and is a perfect example of what saturated color can do for a space. Strong color is a wake-up call, a bold bid for attention that usually works just as intended. For those whose preference for a power punch tends toward deep violet, emerald, indigo, or tangerine, the principle holds equally true, and these hues can deliver the same

# SATURATED
## AND SOFT COLORS

FOR THOSE WHO LOVE STRONG COLOR AND WANT TO INTRODUCE IT INTO THEIR HOME, HARMONY LIES IN SELECTING A BOLD COLOR AND LAYERING WITH CONFIDENCE.

impact. The crucial factors in using a saturated color are the strength and clarity of the hue and the confidence with which you use it. The colors we've chosen to call "soft" are not quite the opposite of saturated; they're more like their kissing cousins. Soft colors are romantic, flattering, and enduring, and include a range drawn from nature's gentler hues: cerulean, lavender, lemon, periwinkle, rose. They layer well with neutrals or with other soft hues of the same value. Soft colors have always been natural choices for the bath, bedroom, and nursery, but you'll also find that they're flattering and fresh in the living room, dining area, or kitchen, too.

# Selecting a Saturated Color Palette

When it comes to using eye-popping color in their homes, most people either wouldn't dream of it or they can't imagine life without it. Bold color is an adventure worth taking, but it requires careful decision making.

For those in search of drama in a room, nothing beats rich, wall-to-wall saturated color. Before you take the plunge, though, try a simple test. Mark off an area of 2–4 square feet (30–120 cm) and paint a color swatch on your wall – preferably on two walls – so you can see how the hue looks under different light conditions, including lamplight. If you are trying to decide between two or more colors, paint swatches in each color to compare. Live with the colors for at least a week to see how they agree with you.

An increasingly popular choice, suited to even more conservative tastes, is to highlight a single wall, an entryway, or an architectural feature with bold color. This trick brings instant energy to a room and has been known to make converts of the most timid home colorists. Another alternative is to start with a less frequently used space such as a dedicated dining room, where the intensity of the color will have a lesser impact than in a room that you use daily.

Whatever size room you choose to paint, balance bold color with lighter elements: white trim or accents in pale or neutral hues, light-colored rugs or wooden floors, furniture upholstered in muted tones. Above all, take care not to overdo saturated color. Stick to just one vibrant color in a room, and consider the views from adjoining rooms as well.

## SATURATED INSPIRATIONS

You're not likely to use a whole range of bold colors within one room. Find samples and swatches that appeal to you that also coordinate with other hues in your decorating plan.

- **PLAN THE AREA** for which you're choosing a saturated color carefully, whether an entire room or just a feature wall. Take into account the impact that amount of color will have on the room.

- **CHOOSE COLORS** for accent pieces that carry color out into the rest of the room. Pillows, throws, and other small accessories, whether solid or patterned, are essential parts of a color plan.

- **CONSIDER FURNITURE FINISHES** when choosing colors, too. Light woods play well off saturated colors; darker ones intensify the color's effect.

York Harbor Yellow 2154-40

Hawthorne Yellow HC-4

Guilford Green HC-116

Sherwood Green HC-118

Spicy Mustard 2154-20

Shelburne Buff HC-28

Alligator Green 2143-20

Guacamole 2144-10

Sangria 2006-20

Peatmoss 2103-30

Cabernet 2116-30

Gentleman's Gray 2062-20

Caramel Latte 2166-20

Deep Poinsettia 2091-30

Van Courtland Blue HC-145

Philipsburg Blue HC-159

**Well-Staged Drama,** *left*

A partial wall like this one, which screens the working part of a kitchen from an open-plan dining area, is a prime candidate for saturated color. Highlighting one single wall with a bold hue is a savvy way to enjoy the benefits of strong color without being overwhelmed by it. Carry the color through the room with decorative accessories like pillows, table settings, or other accent pieces. Red is a perennial favorite, prized for its energizing appeal.

**Pure and Vibrant,** *right*

Yellows are often used for a cheery and charming effect – think of yellow-and-white summer cottages – but a saturated yellow like the marigold featured here can evoke a more cosmopolitan air. If choosing a strong wall color for an entire room, especially a living room, it's often safest to stay away from extremes of color and choose a midtone that delivers impact but still enhances the room's furnishings and lets them retain focus.

**Snug and Stylish,** *left*

Rich saturated hues work as well in smaller spaces as they do in larger ones, especially if you're aiming to create a secluded spot for work or for reading and relaxing. This attic office has a cozy and inviting feel with its plum walls and warm wood furnishings. White-stained woodwork is a smart choice for breaking up and balancing the stronger hues and deeper tones. An abundance of daylight is welcome in any room but is especially important in a room painted in saturated color.

# Selecting a Soft Color Palette

Not to be confused with pastels, soft colors have a crisp appeal all their own. They're also more versatile than you might think, pairing as successfully with stainless steel as they do with white wainscoting.

Once relegated to the bedroom and bath, soft colors are now used to make the living room, dining room, and kitchen look fresh. The way we decorate rooms with soft tones has been updated as well. Pairing a soft wall color with floral fabric is a timeless favorite, but the same color set off by crisp white linen uphol-stery produces an effect that's every bit as welcoming. To make soft colors work in any part of your home, choose slightly grayer counterparts to pastels, which might come off as too sweet or bright.

Like saturated colors, soft colors can benefit from being finished with clean white trim. You can also try tinting white paint with the wall color that you've chosen, to create a paler version of the primary hue for use on trim or ceilings. Using graduated values of a color that you love can help you coordinate adjacent areas. For instance, add white to the color you've chosen for the bedroom and use it on the bathroom walls. Or you might choose a slightly darker shade of the bedroom color for the adjacent hallway. Paint professionals can work with you to assure a pleasing difference in values.

Soft colors work well with silver-toned accessories, from your grandmother's sterling to contemporary steel photo frames. They're also as striking a backdrop for black-and-white photographs as they are for bright artworks and objects in contrasting colors.

SOFT INSPIRATIONS

When choosing soft colors, think "fresh" rather than "delicate." Find colors that recall early spring and summer mornings, and their dusky counterparts.

■ CHOOSE FURNISHINGS that don't necessarily match the wall color but instead are interesting variations or attractive complements.

■ NATURAL MATERIALS like wicker, raffia, linen, and sisal are particularly attractive in a room decorated in a soft palette.

■ CONSIDER COLOR VALUE: Find a hue for a wall color, then choose colors in lighter or darker values of that hue for trim, accents, and fabrics. For contrast, if the wall color is warm, choose some cooler complementary hues and include them in the mix, or vice versa.

| | | | |
|---|---|---|---|
| Filtered Sunlight 2154-60 | Hancock Green HC-117 | Summer Shower 2135-60 | Hint of Violet 2114-60 |
| Weston Flax HC-5 | Hollingsworth Green HC-141 | Blue Hydrangea 2062-60 | Strawberry-N-Cream 2103-70 |
| Philadelphia Cream HC-30 | Soft Fern 2144-40 | Blue Jean 2062-50 | Pale Berry 2103-60 |
| Straw 2154-50 | Castleton Mist HC-1 | Woodlawn Blue HC-147 | Victorian Mauve 2114-50 |
| Beacon Hill Damask HC-2 | Georgian Green HC-115 | Buxton Blue HC-149 | Touch of Gray 2116-60 |
| Dunmore Cream HC-29 | Rosemary Sprig 2144-30 | Jamestown Blue HC-148 | Hazy Lilac 2116-40 |

ATLANTIC

BENJAMIN

COLOR

**Simple Pleasure**, *left*

Sunny flaxen walls pair with milky white trim and warm pine furniture for an enduring color combination that's a pleasure to live with every day. Soft colors are seen more and more these days in living and dining rooms because they add energy and color to a space but are quiet enough to be a flexible backdrop for your decor. The simplicity of this color palette is complemented by a similar restraint in furnishings.

**Neat and Clean**, *right*

Sky blue and white combine to give this tidy laundry room a breezy appeal. The palette is refreshing yet calm, and it welcomes accents in other complementary soft colors — bottle and spring greens, pale grayed blues, creamy beiges — as well as materials such as warm wicker and cool metal.

**Fresh Appeal**, *right*

Soft green hues like this celery offer another lively but adaptable range of colors to choose from. According to color theorists, green is seen as calming, but paired with white cabinetry and trim, it also brings a gentle energy to a room. In this neat and trim family room, the palette is warmed by natural wood, wicker, sisal, and cotton twill, and punctuated with a few bursts of stronger color in the throw pillows and accent pieces.

The special virtues of pattern are well known: patterns give a room its character and depth, and help define its overall style. They express exuberance, come in countless varieties – dots, florals, graphics, paisleys, and stripes of all sizes – and effortlessly multiply their effect when mixed in artistic combination. Because they can be used to great advantage in small quantities, patterns are also immensely practical. The punch they bring to a room frees you to opt for solid colored fabrics for basic

# PATTERN
## AND TEXTURE

PATTERN AND TEXTURE ARE THE UNDERAPPRECIATED SUPPORTING PLAYERS OF HOME DESIGN, ADDING INTEREST AND PERSONALITY WITHOUT STEALING THE SCENE.

upholstery and drapes, and to choose pillows, throws, and area rugs in more daring designs for fresh impact or an occasional update. Texture, pattern's close relation, enhances visual appeal in a room, upping its luxury quotient with the addition of brushed canvas, fur, silk, and velvet, or relaxing more formal furnishings by contrasting them with a rustic basket, handwoven rug, or stone bowl. Bringing texture into a room is like inviting good conversationalists to a dinner party. Just as you'd gather a mix of interesting friends at the table to spark one another, bring together multiple textures in your home to create an intriguing atmosphere.

# Adding Pattern and Texture

One of the pleasures of using pattern and texture in a room is the license it gives you to indulge your taste for variety and whimsy while maintaining an overall sense of harmony.

As with most seemingly effortless effects, the secret to successfully mixing pattern and texture lies in understanding some basic principles before you begin tweaking them. The photo grid at right illustrates a simple but almost foolproof method to help you gain confidence in mixing patterns. Group fabrics into categories: solids, overall prints, stripes, geometric prints, and organic prints (shown here in rows of yellows, blues, and reds). When choosing furnishings for a room, look for patterns that share a common color, and pick one from each of these categories. For a livelier effect, you can stray outside the color range, but then it's best to find patterns whose sizes are closely matched. Solid fabrics that read as pattern are also great choices because they harmonize effortlessly: brocades, damasks, herringbones. Smocked, ruched, pleated, or embroidered fabrics also read as pattern and are easy to include in a mix.

Translate these same principles to the entire room. For example, you might have a mix of solid upholstery, geometric rugs, and subtly striped draperies. You might add side chairs upholstered in a small overall pattern and throw pillows of an organic pattern.

Once you have your furniture in place, begin to explore textural variations that add visual interest. Start with contrasts: shiny silk with matte velvet; nubby chenille with smooth leather; glazed porcelain with rustic wood. Try out different patterns and textures, adding and subtracting a piece at a time until you've got the perfect mix.

**Solids**
The solid piece of the mix may be your upholstery or bed covering, whether classic linen or soft leather. For greater depth, look for solid fabrics with strong tactile interest: mohair, chenille, matelassé, or ruched or pleated fabrics.

**Overall Prints**
Small motifs repeated over large areas create overall pattern, which is surprisingly versatile when used in a mix. Quilted and embroidered fabrics, particularly in small repeated designs, display pattern through texture.

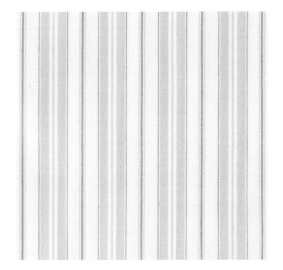

### Stripes

Perhaps the most versatile of all patterns, stripes come in a great range of widths and colors, from narrow ticking to broad awning stripes, making them friendly companions to many other fabric patterns.

### Geometric Prints

Another extremely easy mixer, geometrics include an enormous range of patterns, from simple checks and plaids to the more complicated angular patterns found in kilim rugs and upholstery and carpet materials.

### Organic Prints

Flowing vines, florals, and many other patterns that take inspiration from the natural world mix well with many other patterns and bring vitality to a grouping. Organic patterns add richness and romance to a setting.

**Layered Comfort,** *left*
This rich mix of patterns and textures conjures the feel of an exotic spa. Deftly juxtaposing smooth and polished surfaces with rough and honed ones, the decor demonstrates how texture and pattern play off each other – the geometry of the kilims is balanced with the repeated pattern of the iron grille, the filmy voile at the window contrasts with the rough stone and cast-earth walls. Furnishings are harmonized by their earthy and jewel-tone colors.

**Quiet Pattern,** *right*
A subtle combination of patterns brings an elegant sophistication to a grouping. A mix of pillows with their small repeated motifs is united by their similar colors; the carpet plays out the colors in a larger motif. The throw's nubby weave adds another layer of texture and also reads as pattern. Contrasts in texture also add appeal – the sheen of silk and leather against the soft basketweave of the upholstery.

**Easy Comfort,** *left*
Layers of texture make even a simple, casual room more interesting and engaging. Here, a cream, blue, and brown palette looks polished and inviting thanks to the understated mix of patterns and textures. The visible weave of the sofa fabric contrasts with the plush pick-stitch quilt and downy throw. Pillows play by the rules and mix a solid, stripe, and pattern, but all stay within the palette.

LIGHT

"SUNLIGHT CHANGES THE WHOLE FEELING OF MY HOME. I WANT A BALANCED MIX OF LIGHTING THAT SUSTAINS THAT WARMTH BUT LETS ME CREATE DIFFERENT MOODS."

Natural light is universally welcomed in our everyday lives. We still turn the clocks back each autumn to buy back that single hour of morning sun. In the home, windows, skylights, French doors, and doors with side lights are the primary portals of daylight, and they're the best starting points for developing a lighting plan for your house. When choosing window treatments, think not only of their decorative effects, but also look at them as opportunities to control the quantity and

# WORKING WITH
# NATURAL LIGHT

NATURAL SUNLIGHT INFUSES A ROOM WITH LIFE. USE IT AS A POWERFUL TOOL TO TRANSFORM COLORS, WARM THE ATMOSPHERE, AND LIGHTEN THE HEART.

quality of illumination in your home. There's something comforting about the dappled patterns thrown across furnishings by sunlight peeking through Venetian blinds; the sheerest of fabrics at the window filters the sun's rays while still preserving views beyond. On those mornings when you don't want sunbeams breaking into your bedroom, lined draperies or blackout shades save the day. Beyond the control of light, fabric draperies also help soften rooms full of hard surfaces, such as the dining room. When a room calls for restraint, blinds, shades, and shutters offer tailored alternatives, and also contribute a sense of architectural character.

# Fabric at the Window

Well-chosen draperies can do for a room what a colorful scarf does for an everyday outfit. Use simple panels of fabric to add instant texture and color.

Simple fabric panels hanging gracefully from iron or wood rods are the standard for window treatments today. Not only do they make decorating simpler than treatments with valances and swags, they also are less expensive, and there's a broad selection available ready-made. Use them to add color and textural interest to any room.

Draperies can be lined or unlined, paired with sheers, or hung on their own. Unlined draperies have a loose, natural drape and allow some daylight to filter through them. Combining sheer panels of voile or organdy with opaque draperies provides the maximum amount of privacy and flexibility in controlling the amount of light that a room gets. Translucent fabrics like linen, organdy, and voile gently filter light without blocking views. Heavier fabrics such as velvet are more formal looking but effectively block sun in summer and drafts in winter.

Draperies in a solid color or understated stripes create a more enduring background for a room than drapes with a showy print. Choosing a drapery color in a shade close to that of the walls is a sophisticated way to dress up a room. Single-toned damasks or raw silks add textural interest and natural elegance to an otherwise spare setting. Whatever your choice of fabric, hanging draperies high on a wall is a simple way to add height and grace to a room.

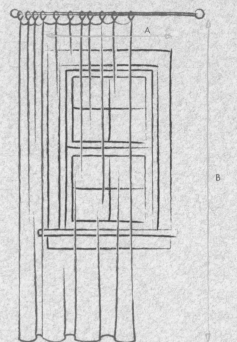

## MEASURING FOR DRAPERIES

A good rule of thumb is to mount rods 4" (10 cm) above a window frame. You can add visual height to a room by mounting a rod just below the ceiling moulding (or ceiling). Another attractive option is to place the rod midway between ceiling and top of window.

■ ROD LENGTH: A pole or rod should extend 3–6" (7.5–15 cm) beyond both sides of the window frame if you want open draperies to completely clear the window. Always decide on the type of rod, its mounted height, and hanging method (see opposite page) before measuring for draperies, because these affect final measurements.

■ DRAPERY LENGTH: Measure the distance from the rod to the floor (B). Floor-length curtains should clear the floor by 1" (2.5 cm). For a puddle effect, add 6–8" (15–20 cm) to the rod-to-floor measurement. For draperies that just break at the floor, add 3–4" (7.5–10 cm). Factor in the size of the pole and rings, tie tops, or clips, as these can add 1" (2.5 cm) or more to the hanging length.

■ DRAPERY WIDTH: Measure the width of the window including the frame (A) and multiply by 1 for a tailored look, by 1.5 for a standard look, or by 3 for a full look. The lighter the fabric, the more you'll need to achieve a full look.

Sheer panels, *left*, are gathered at the bottoms and pinned up to the center with a ribbon, a simple way to dress up lightweight draperies.

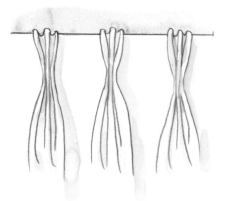

### Track-Rod Mount

A rod that contains a track allows you to draw draperies easily with string controls on the side. Utilitarian in looks, track-rods are concealed by the drapery heading (in this case, pinched pleats).

### Pole Pocket Mount

A fabric pocket across the top of a panel creates a channel through which a pole is inserted. This style calls for a full look, and because it can be difficult to draw drapes, it is most suitable for sheers.

### Ring-Top and Pole Mount

This style is a favorite for its casual look and also for the ease with which draperies can be opened and closed. Almost any type of fabric works with this informal mounting.

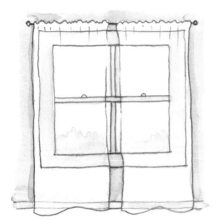

### Sheer Fabrics

Fabrics such as voile, organdy, and handkerchief linen offer an airy feel. They reduce glare while maintaining the view, but they do not provide much privacy at night.

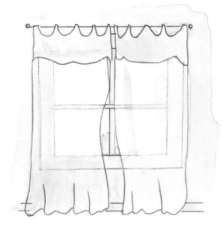

### Unlined Fabrics

Medium-weight fabrics such as linen or cotton do not necessarily require lining. Unlined cottons and linens offer both privacy and light, and are a good choice for a more casual look.

### Lined Fabrics

Heavier fabrics such as raw silk and velvet are traditionally lined to help screen out light and noise. Plan for a 3" (7.5 cm) overlap in the middle to create a continuous screen across the window.

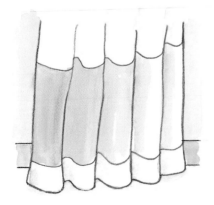

### Border Upgrade

Ready-made draperies can be customized with a distinctive sewn-on border. A border may be a contrasting solid fabric or print and should not exceed one-third of the drapery's length.

### Contrast Lining

A patterned or contrasting-color lining adds panache to solid-color draperies. It's not necessary to line the entire curtain; an 18" (45 cm) strip along the center edges will give the look of a full lining.

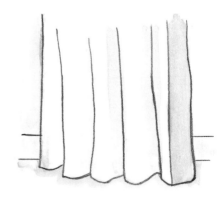

### Contrast Edging

A band of ribbon or a strip of fabric in a color contrasting to the drapery fabric can be sewn onto the edges of panels to give them a tailored finish and add an extra touch of color.

# Blinds, Shades, and Shutters

Generally more casual than draperies, this group of sleek window coverings can be used in conjunction with draperies for maximum control of light and privacy.

Sometimes even the most informal draperies just don't work in a given room or on a particular window. It may be because of an architectural element – a built-in window seat or a radiator, for example – or because of practical concerns or style preferences. Children's rooms, for instance, are best served by contained window treatments, especially blackout shades, which are a great help with early bedtimes. (Look for a cordless lift option, which is safer around children and pets.) In terms of style, the more casual the room, the more one is inclined to choose blinds or shutters for its window dressing.

Within the wide world of blinds, shades, and shutters, your choice should be guided by the style and material that best complement other elements in the room as well as by your goals for light and privacy (information in the adjacent box and on the opposite page will help you evaluate your options). Fabric may be preferred, to soften a room or to coordinate with other furnishings; use Venetian blinds or shutters to add architectural interest to a plain space. Natural woven window treatments – grasses, reeds, matchstick, and bamboo – are suitable even in dressy settings and instantly bring contrast to any room. They contribute texture both through their materials and with the light patterns they create. Panel track blinds, available in a variety of fabrics and materials, are a sleek new style that offer privacy and effectively block sunlight.

## MEASURING FOR BLINDS & SHADES

Careful measuring is essential when ordering blinds, shades, or shutters. Use a metal tape measure, not a cloth one, which has too much give. Measure all windows separately because dimensions may vary slightly.

■ INSIDE MOUNTING: An inside mount makes a neat, tailored impression but is suitable only for window frames with enough depth to accommodate the blind or shutter completely within them. The depth must be at least 2" (5 cm) for blinds and can be more, depending on the thickness of the blind. Most shutters require a depth of 2 ½" (6 cm) inside the frame. Windows must also be square, with no warping. To test for squareness, measure the inside of the window diagonally in both directions. If there is a difference of more than ½" (13 mm) between the measurements, the window is not square and you should mount outside the frame.

If your window is suitable for an inside mount, measure the width (A) in several different places. Repeat with the height (B), measuring on both sides and at the center point. Always use the narrowest measurement to ensure a clean fit.

■ OUTSIDE MOUNTING: For windows in poor condition, unattractively framed windows, or windows where there is too little depth for an interior mount, it's best to mount treatments outside the frame. Measure width (C) and height (D) as above, and add 3 ¼" (8 cm) to both measurements. A flat wall surface around the opening of at least 1 ⅝" (4 cm) is needed for an outside mount.

A relaxed Roman shade, *left*, is a fitting choice for a window over a built-in seat. Feel free to mix shades and draperies within the same room.

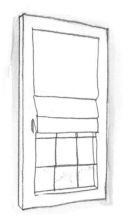

**Roman Shade**

Tailored treatments that pull up in flat folds, Roman shades can be fitted inside or outside the window frame. They work well with a variety of fabrics, from sheer linen to heavyweight canvas.

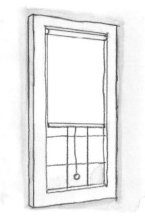

**Roller Shade**

The simplest type of retractable opaque blind, fabric roller shades can be found ready-made in basic colors or can be custom ordered to match your wall color or upholstery.

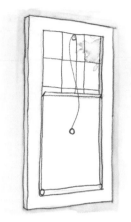

**Bottom-Up Shade**

A popular design for urban living, these ensure privacy while admitting light through the upper portion. They're available in bottom-mounted roller designs and also in custom materials.

**Honeycomb Shade**

Honeycomb and pleated shades, made from materials and fabrics designed to hold their pleats permanently, are softer than standard blinds and admit light through their translucent materials.

**Venetian Blind**

This classic style remains popular due to its versatility. Venetian blinds provide privacy and excellent light control, and cast attractive patterns of sunlight and shadow.

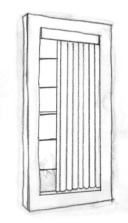

**Vertical Blind**

Similar to panel track blinds, vertical vanes 3 ½" (8 cm) wide slide on a track and stack to one side. They're a good solution for large windows and sliding doors and are available in various lengths.

**Panel Track**

Useful for windows or sliding glass doors, these vertical panels 8–18" (20–45 cm) wide, made of fabric or natural woven material, slide on a track and stack to one side when open.

**Louvered Shutter**

Slatted shutters can be adjusted to admit as much light as desired, though they do not close tightly enough to block light out completely. Made of wood or synthetics, they can be stained or painted.

**Paneled Shutter**

Solid wooden shutters are a smart choice in cities, where street noise is an issue; in cold climates, where they provide insulation; and in children's bedrooms, where they block out light and sound.

**Asymmetrical Elegance**, *left*
Even formal window treatments like this velvet and embroidered voile pairing take on a more offhand air when given an unexpected, asymmetrical treatment. Here, two velvet panels are pulled to one side and tied back with a pepperberry spray. A single panel of embroidered voile on the back rod is pulled neatly across the window to filter incoming daylight.

**Simple and Striking**, *right*
If you have a light and airy room and want to preserve that sense of openness, Roman shades are a great option. They offer a polished look and effective light control, but keep a window looking neat and leave window mouldings and walls unadorned. Roman shades are available in a wide array of materials and fabrics, either ready-made or customized to match upholstery or wall color. Here, bold stripes make a strong statement and add punch to a white room.

The way that we perceive a room – as restful, romantic, welcoming, or cold – depends very much on how it is lit. It's helpful to understand the three main types of lighting – ambient, task, and accent – so that you can use them to best effect. Ambient light is generally the available natural light during the day; at night it's usually provided by a central overhead fixture, lamps, or a group of recessed lights that evenly illuminate an entire room. Task lighting is self-explanatory, directing light for

# WORKING WITH
# LIGHTING

LAMPLIGHT EXTENDS OUR DAYS, AIDS OUR EYESIGHT, AND INFLUENCES OUR MOODS. NO SINGLE SOURCE WORKS ON ITS OWN, SO PLAN FOR A DIVERSE, BALANCED MIX.

specific activities. Accent lights are the jewelry of a room – the spots, candles, and picture lights that add sparkle. But all lighting fixtures can add to a room's style. A reading lamp with an opaque shade throws strong light onto the tabletop, calling attention to a featured object and serving as accent as well as task lighting. Recessed ceiling fixtures can be fitted with wall-washer bulbs or with spots that call attention to an architectural feature, a work of art, or a whole bookcase. A small chandelier can deliver part of a room's ambient light while serving as a dramatic focal point. Use function and style together to achieve the best effect.

# Day to Night

Light is never constant. It shifts by the second, transforming an interior space, and our moods along with it. Celebrate the evening by orchestrating your own effects.

A bright, open space by day can seem a more intimate and secluded spot by night with the simple flip of a switch. It's human nature to be drawn to light as the sky darkens and rooms grow dimmer with the setting sun. In colder seasons we gather around the fireplace for both light and warmth. But summer months benefit from flickering flames as well, in the form of candles, which also draw guests together. Make the most of a seating group already arranged around a fireplace and add votives on the cocktail table, or dramatize the moment with a collection of grand tapers in assorted candlesticks on the mantel. Candlelight and firelight are known as "kinetic light," which has special appeal because of its movement. Supplement its enchanting attraction with low levels of ambient lighting, to create a more comfortable light balance within the room and prevent potential mishaps as people move around.

**This open-plan room**, *right and opposite page,* is lit by a skylight and floor-to-ceiling windows by day. At night, a floor lamp and a recessed spotlight on the mantel provide illumination; votive candles reflected on lustrous surfaces set a festive mood.

## DESIGN LESSON THE COLOR OF LIGHT

Understanding that different kinds of light bulbs emit slightly different colors of light is critical to planning flattering lighting for your home. Lamps that give off a warmer color enhance skin tones, putting you and your guests in a better light. Whiter light is better for task work like reading and for illuminating artwork. Full-spectrum light is most like natural light and is quite versatile. Painted walls are especially affected by lighting's color, so it's important to evaluate sample wall colors in artificial light, particularly for dining rooms and bedrooms, which are so often used at night.

■ INCANDESCENT LIGHT is warm and flatters the skin. Easily controlled by dimmers or with three-way bulbs, it is versatile enough to be used for ambient, task, or accent lighting.

■ HALOGEN BULBS produce the whitest light of any bulb and thus do not influence the color of furnishings or art. They're considered the best choice for task lighting.

■ FLUORESCENT LIGHT, which had a bad name in the past, is now often color-corrected to simulate daylight. The most energy-efficient of all lamps, fluorescents are available in standard tubes as well as in bulbs that fit screw-in sockets.

# Lamps

The role of lamps in balancing the lighting of any room is critical because they offer the ultimate flexibility to supplement built-in fixtures.

The most comfortable rooms are those that evenly balance light from diverse sources. Ideally, light sources within one room sit at different levels. Ambient lighting tends to come from the ceiling; table and floor lamps bring spots of light into the center of the space, helping to disperse light throughout the room; accent lights are most often directed toward a wall, a mantel, or another architectural feature, or are focused on a painting or sculptural object. A lamp's shade is also an influence on a harmonious lighting plan. An opaque or semi-opaque shade is not only a stylish choice but also is recommended for reading because it focuses light onto a page. Lamps arranged around a conversation seating area may cast a more diffuse light and so should be dressed accordingly. Translucent vellum shades give off a soft golden glow; silk shades lined with fabric cast an especially gentle and flattering light and create a sense of intimacy in a room.

Within the same space, lamps need not match but should be of compatible styles. Choosing shades in a single palette will unify a grouping of different lamps. If you'd like to feature one unique decorative lamp and give it focus, choose more understated styles for other lamps in the room, such as a pharmacy-style lamp, which seems almost to disappear. Sometimes a shaded lamp that sits in the center of a room can be a visual barrier, whereas a slim-profile lamp will tend to open up a space.

ROOM-BY-ROOM SOLUTIONS

The most harmonious lighting plans include different sources of light, such as a central fixture or recessed lights in the ceiling, table lamps around the room, and directional spots on the walls. Providing lamps at different levels evenly disperses light. In general, the more sources of light there are, the less contrast there will be, as it's easier to achieve a balanced distribution.

■ LIVING ROOM: Central ceiling fixtures are less common now, so ambient light is best achieved with recessed can lights. Some cans should have directional bulbs aimed over the mantel and at walls, bookcases, or art. If recessed lights are not an option, consider track lighting. Add lamps at table and floor heights. Lamps included in a room for task lighting also add to the ambient light.

■ DINING ROOM: A chandelier controlled by a dimmer may be the centerpiece of the plan, but it should not be the only source of light. Use candles and wall sconces or table lamps on a buffet to balance the light. Recessed lights fitted with low-voltage halogen spots can create dramatic accent lighting when focused on artworks.

■ KITCHEN: This space requires plenty of both ambient and task lighting. Work surfaces require good lighting without glare; recessed downlights set about 12" (30 cm) out from the overhead cabinets are efficent for providing illumination on the front of base cabinets. If possible, supplement these with under-counter lighting fitted with fluorescent or halogen bulbs. Recessed downlights adequately light an island unless the ceiling is more than 10' (3 m) high; pendants that bring the light closer to the work surface are best used with higher or vaulted ceilings. In an open-plan kitchen, put all lights on dimmers so that you can subdue the kitchen lights while dining.

■ BEDROOM: This resting place calls for gentle ambient light from overhead fixtures combined with specific task lighting, especially for reading. Well-placed accent lights create a romantic mood. Don't forget to adequately light the closet.

■ BATHROOM: Be kind to yourself and guests in lighting the bath and powder room. Keep the ambient light soft and flattering, and address specific areas such as tub and shower with attractive task lighting.

An opaque shade, *left*, turns a decorative task lamp into an accent light, casting directional light that illuminates table accessories.

### Work Light

An adjustable-arm work lamp is a longtime favorite that allows you to direct light just where you want it. The ideal height puts the bottom of the lampshade at eye level or just below. See other desk lamp options below.

### Bedside Lamp

Recommended height for a bedside lamp is 20" (51 cm) from your pillow to the bottom of the shade. A relatively opaque shade helps concentrate light on the page. See more options for bedside lighting below.

### Floor Lamp

Light from a floor lamp should fall unobstructed over your shoulder. For lamps at the side of a chair, the distance from floor to bottom of shade should be 40–42" (102–107 cm), or at about eye level. See another chairside option below.

### Vintage-style Desk Lamp

A crook-arm–style lamp with a metal shade makes a stylish alternative to an adjustable lamp on a small desk, but it has a more limited range of illumination and therefore requires especially good ambient light to accompany it.

### Swing-Arm Wall Fixture

A popular alternative to the bedside table lamp, the swing-arm lamp offers greater flexibility in positioning the light for reading and frees up space on the nightstand. Most swing-arm fixtures are hard-wired and so must be custom fit.

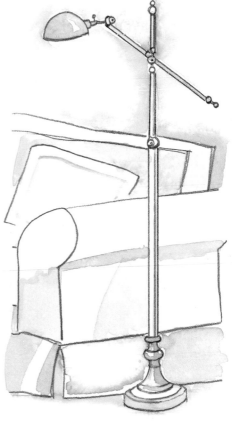

### Table Lamp

The bottom of a table lamp's shade should be about 15" (38 cm) above the desk surface for optimal reading light. A translucent shade helps eliminate glare and contributes to a room's ambient light while still serving as task lighting.

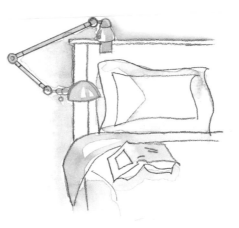

### Adjustable-Arm Clip-on Lamp

An adjustable clip-on lamp makes an economic and stylish bedside lamp when attached to a headboard or a bedside table. You can control both its horizontal and vertical position and the span of light that it casts.

### Swing-Arm Pharmacy Lamp

An adjustable lamp allows each family member to position the light exactly at their eye level for reading. Its slim profile makes it unobtrusive. Aim the bowl toward a wall or turn it up to the ceiling for ambient lighting.

### A Balanced Mix, *left*

Gradations of light give a room greater depth. Multiple sources of light are well balanced here, from the hanging drum shades to votives clustered on the table and pillar candles on the mantel. As night falls and guests gather, the effect becomes more dramatic. Light draws attention wherever it is placed or focused, so keep a room visually lively with thoughtful placement of sources and gleaming surfaces to catch and reflect it.

### Warm and Welcoming, *right*

Electric- and candlelight combine to give this tailored living room a welcoming atmosphere. The translucent shade of a floor lamp casts a warm glow while the opaque shade on the wall sconce focuses light on the wall and mantel below. A white vase in the mantel grouping holds a votive candle in a nice counterpoint to the sconce; tapers on the coffee table bring a glow to the center of the room.

### Multiuse Versatility, *left*

This combination family room—home office space benefits from a well-designed lighting plan. Dimmable halogen wall fixtures can be turned upward to provide an ambient wash or downward to focus on the photographs and illuminate the desk and sofa. The articulated desk lamp can be adjusted for users at the sofa or worktable. Both demonstrate how task lighting also contributes to a room's ambient lighting.

MATERIALS

kona solid hardwood flooring

laminate flooring in walnut

engineered flooring in stained oak

bamboo flooring

# Guide to Materials

Whether you are redecorating your entire home or simply sprucing up a room, choosing materials is a key step in the process. The right materials achieve the look you want, prove practical for your uses, and meet your budget requirements.

## Flooring

**Solid wood flooring** *(pictured above)* is available in a variety of species, from traditional red oak to Brazilian cherry and salvaged pine. Prices vary considerably, with domestic species like oak and maple at the low end of the price ladder and less abundant exotics at the top. Wood can be stained to just about any color, and it can be re-sanded and refinished when it begins to look worn. Lighter woods lend themselves to casual decorating styles, while darker woods, such as walnut or wenge, suggest more formal interiors. Strip flooring comes in a few standard widths, starting at 2 ¼" (6 cm). Planks of pine, walnut, and other wood species up to 20" (51 cm) wide also are available (expect to pay a premium for those). Flooring can be finished on-site, or at the factory before installation (see Flooring Finishes for Wood, page 358).

**Laminate flooring** *(pictured above)* is made to look like wood flooring, but it's actually a high-tech marriage of fiberboard and a thin, photo-like layer protected by a clear plastic film. It is often used in mudrooms and entryways or in commercial applications. Less expensive than conventional wood

flooring, laminate flooring is made by a number of companies and is easy to find at home centers. You can install laminate flooring yourself without hiring a professional. Newer versions come in a number of wood tones and have guarantees of up to 25 years. Unlike wood, a laminate floor can't be refinished.

**Engineered flooring** *(pictured above)* is made from several thin sheets of wood that are glued together to make a plank. It works in places that solid wood flooring can't, such as a basement, where it can be placed directly over concrete. The top layer can be a different wood species than the rest of the plank, allowing manufacturers to offer a range of woods. Most engineered flooring comes already finished, and some brands have a thick enough top layer to be re-sanded just like solid wood flooring. Another advantage: planks come in widths up to 7" (18 cm). The best grades are comparable in cost to conventional solid wood. Brand names include Armstrong, Eco Timber, Waverly, Max Windsor, and Robbins.

**Bamboo flooring** *(pictured above)* is quickly gaining popularity for its light, natural coloring and attractive texture. Bamboo flooring also makes

environmental sense because it's made from a fast-growing plant that's ready to harvest in as little as four years. After harvesting, bamboo stalks are cut into strips and then laminated into pieces of flooring as durable as oak. Bamboo can be ordered unfinished or factory finished. Because it doesn't shrink and expand as much as solid wood flooring, it's a good choice over radiant-floor heating systems. Bamboo can be used in any room of the house, but take care in a bathroom or other wet areas: like solid wood flooring, bamboo can be damaged by water.

**Rubber flooring** is more often seen in commercial or industrial settings, but it's also an option where its durability and resilience underfoot make it a practical choice, such as in a kitchen, home gym, or playroom. Rubber flooring is available in sheet and tile forms. Varieties with surface textures have more slip resistance than plain flooring and are often specified for contemporary kitchens because they're both stylish and easy on the feet. Selection is somewhat limited. Rubber flooring is comparable in cost to good-quality vinyl, and less expensive than solid or engineered wood flooring and many types of ceramic and stone tile.

**Cork flooring** is enjoying a resurgence of interest, in part because it's a natural product made from a renewable resource and because modern finishes have made maintenance easier. Available in tile or plank form, cork is a resilient floor that's warm and comfortable underfoot. Cork should be sealed after installation, and the finish will need periodic maintenance. It's available in several densities, with higher densities contributing to longer

wear. Like wood, cork expands and contracts with moisture, so it's not the best choice for a bathroom, laundry, or utility room. When used in the kitchen, high-wear work areas should be protected with rugs. Cork is comparable in cost to moderately priced wood.

**Linoleum flooring** is an old-fashioned favorite made from renewable resources including wood flour, linseed oil, and ground limestone. Durable, resilient, and comfortable underfoot, it's available in many colors and patterns, in sheet form as well as tiles. Although vinyl largely displaced linoleum because it didn't need as much maintenance, newer versions of linoleum do not require waxing. Linoleum costs more than most vinyl and should be installed professionally.

**Vinyl** remains a popular resilient flooring, in part because it needs very little maintenance. The patterns on inlaid vinyl go all the way through the material so they don't wear off. More expensive versions have a top surface, called the wear layer, made with extremely tough materials like aluminum oxide to withstand heavy foot traffic. Prices vary considerably, but economical varieties are among the least expensive flooring options available.

**Natural stone tile** is available in many materials, including limestone, slate, soapstone, marble, and granite. Stone makes a durable, naturally beautiful flooring material that doesn't need much maintenance. Because of its density, stone is a good choice over radiant-floor heating systems, and it stays cool underfoot in warm weather. All stone, with the exception of soapstone, should be sealed

cast-earth flooring

undermount sink

pedestal sink

apron-front sink

to prevent staining and may require periodic re-sealing. Stone tile, like ceramic tile, shouldn't be installed over a bouncy subfloor, so existing floors may need reinforcing if you're thinking of re-flooring with tile. Stone flooring typically costs more than ceramic tile, and it can be quite expensive.

**Ceramic tile** is available in many colors, textures, and sizes — from small mosaics to pieces up to 18" (45 cm) square — making it an attractive and less costly alternative to natural stone. Glazed ceramic tile requires no sealing and no maintenance beyond regular sweeping and washing. Textured surfaces and unglazed tile are not as slippery as smooth, glazed surfaces. For wet areas like the bathroom, look for a tile with slip resistance. Tile absorbs heat, so it's a good choice over radiant-floor heating systems.

**Handmade clay pavers** in characteristic earth tones, such as the clay Saltillo tiles made in Mexico, are typically air-dried and then fired at low temperatures. They have pleasing variations in thickness, flatness, and coloration. Because they are porous, these pavers should be sealed and are not considered suitable for wet locations. Cast-earth flooring tiles *(pictured above)* are created by pouring a mixture of earth, water, and cement into molds to make a highly insulating material.

**Concrete**, long used for garage and basement slabs, is enjoying new popularity as a finish floor in the rest of the house. It's just as hard-wearing as ceramic tile and can be treated with stains and colorants to produce a range of surface appearances that may surprise you. Concrete is a naturally porous material that must be

sealed to resist stains, but it also can be enlivened with a variety of decorative inlays — metal, wood, even seashells. Like tile and stone floor surfaces, concrete is a natural fit with radiant-floor heat. But it's also heavy, something to take into account when planning. Concrete floors vary quite a bit in cost, depending on how the surface is finished, but they are typically less expensive than stone.

**Brick** makes an extremely durable, colorfast floor surface. Thin clay brick designed especially for interior flooring is installed like ceramic tile and is avail-able in more than a dozen colors. Their surface texture gives them good slip re-sistance, and they can be set in a variety of decorative patterns. Brick tiles vary in size, so a fairly wide grout joint may be recommended. Sealing brick makes it easier to maintain. Prices are comparable to many kinds of ceramic tile.

## Flooring Finishes for Wood

**Oil-modified polyurethane** is a tough, long-wearing floor finish whose ingred-ients impart a characteristic amber color to wood flooring. It's especially noticeable on floors made of lighter woods. Oil-based finishes generally cost less than water-based finishes, but they take longer to dry, and the volatile organic compounds (VOCs) they contain give off an odor as they cure. The good news is that it takes fewer coats of finish to complete the job.

**Water-based urethane** floor finishes are water clear, so they don't give wood the same amber cast that oil-based finishes do. They dry faster than oil-modified urethanes, and they don't give off the

same odor. For all of these reasons, water-based finishes are becoming more widely used, even if they are trickier to apply. On the downside, they typically cost more and it may take more coats to get the same level of protection.

**Pre-finished flooring** gets a protective coating at the factory, so you don't have to sand, seal, or apply a protective finish after flooring is installed. Factory finishes are applied to many brands of wood and engineered wood flooring. Formulations may contain tough ceramic particles for long wear — and long warranties.

## Kitchen and Bath Sinks

### Types of Sinks

Sinks for kitchens and bathrooms are no longer a design afterthought. New shapes, materials, and colors allow hardworking sinks to make a style state-ment. There are three key factors in choosing a sink: what it's made from, how big it is, and how it will be in-stalled. In the kitchen, the standard is a 33" x 22" (84 x 56 cm) two-bowl design that fits in a 36"-wide (90 cm) sink cabinet. But many other sizes are available, including models with extra-deep 11" (28 cm) bowls that make washing big pots and pans much easier.

**Undermount sinks** *(pictured above)* leave an easy-to-clean, uninterrupted counter surface because there's no sink rim to collect debris. Undermounts work best with countertops made from a solid material, such as stone or concrete, but don't lend themselves to plastic laminate counters because the sink cutout leaves edges of the counter substrate exposed.

**Self-rimming sinks** sit atop the counter, so they can be used with any kind of countertop material. Because the sink's rim can trap food and water, it's not as easy to keep clean as an undermount sink.

**Flush-mount sinks** are much like self-rimming sinks except that the lip of the sink is designed to sit flush with a surrounding tile counter. They have the same advantages of an undermount sink because there's no lip at the edge of the sink to catch crumbs or water. Like self-rimming sinks, they should be sealed to the countertop to prevent leaks.

**Integral sinks** are part of the countertop itself. They can be fabricated from solid surface material (such as DuPont's Corian) and glued into the countertop, or made from stainless steel and welded into a stainless countertop — just like you'd find in a commercial kitchen.

**Pedestal sinks** *(pictured above)*, a bathroom classic, take up less room than a conventional sink and vanity, an advantage in a small bath. They don't provide as much storage space, but a narrow shelf over the sink can help. Most if not all pedestal sinks are vitreous china, made by firing glazed clay at a high temperature to produce a nonporous surface.

**Apron-front sinks** *(pictured above)*, sometimes called farmers' sinks, come in a variety of materials, including stone, fire clay, and porcelain over cast iron. What they have in common is a broad front face that is left exposed by special sink cabinetry. The look has a pleasing vintage flavor to it, not unlike the shallow slate sinks that once were common in farmhouses. Apron-front sinks are a good match for casual, country-style kitchens.

stainless steel countertop

granite countertop

limestone countertop

maple butcher-block countertop

## Sink Materials

**Stainless steel** is the most popular material for kitchen sinks. It has a number of advantages: it won't absorb food or bacteria, doesn't rust, is unaffected by heat, and is relatively easy to clean. Basic stainless steel sinks are made from 20- or 22-gauge metal; better grades are made from 18-gauge or even 16-gauge steel. Brushed and polished finishes are available. Prices vary considerably.

**Fire-clay, or vitreous china,** sinks are made from a durable, high-temperature ceramic material. They are the same all the way through, so a chip won't uncover an underlying layer of metal that can rust. Their smooth surfaces may look something like porcelain, but fire-clay sinks can be finely detailed with surface decoration or paint before they are fired, giving them unique decorative characteristics. Basic fire-clay sinks are competitive in cost with other types, although elaborately detailed models can be quite expensive.

**Porcelain over cast iron** is a time-tested combination that many of us may remember from our grandmother's kitchen. With proper care, the porcelain top surface is very durable but can be damaged by abrasive cleaners. The cast-iron core has good thermal retention once it's been warmed up, and the mass of these sinks makes them quiet when water is running or when they're equipped with a waste disposer. Basic two-bowl models are relatively low in cost. Enameled steel sinks are a lighter, less expensive option, but they are known to chip more easily than porcelain sinks.

**Copper and bronze** sinks are among the most expensive sink options, but these noncorroding metals are very durable and have an appealing rustic character. Copper, the less expensive of the two, needs regular cleaning to look its best. Bronze develops a darker surface patina.

**Vessel sinks** in the bathroom may remind you of an old-fashioned wash basin set atop a chest of drawers. Many are designed to sit on top of a bath vanity, but wall-mounted models also are available. There are many materials to choose from, including tempered glass, ceramic, copper, bronze, and stone. Vessel sinks can become a design focal point in a bath. Because the walls of the sink rise above the counter, one consideration is the height of the bath vanity on which it sits. A higher sink may make life a little easier for anyone who hates to stoop over a conventional sink, but not as convenient for children. Vessel sinks may be fitted with wall-mounted or extra-tall faucets.

## Kitchen Countertops

**Plastic laminate** is an economical countertop choice available in a huge variety of colors and patterns. It's not as heat resistant as other materials and will be damaged by sharp knives, but it's a long-wearing material that requires practically no maintenance and is easy to keep clean. Laminate can be bought in sheet form and installed over a particleboard substrate, or bought as a "post-formed" counter with an integral backsplash and a rolled front edge that's ready for installation. One common objection to laminate is a dark line where the top meets the outside edge, but there are several ways of avoiding it. One is to use a type of laminate that has solid color throughout, such as Formica's ColorCore. Another is to ask the installer to add wood or beveled laminate edgings, which completely disguise the seam.

**Stainless steel and other metals** can be fashioned into very durable, heat-resistant countertops. Stainless steel *(pictured above)* is nonabsorptive and easy to keep clean (one reason it's the standard in commercial kitchens), and a countertop can be made with an integral sink of the same material. Thicker sheets are better at resisting dents. Stainless steel can be scratched, but in time these minor imperfections blend together to create a pleasing patina. Stainless is a moderately expensive countertop choice.

**Ceramic tile** countertops, just like tile floors, are highly resistant to wear, and the tremendous variety in tile colors, patterns, and textures opens the door to virtually unlimited design possibilities. Tile is heat resistant and fairly easy to install. A tile countertop, however, is hard and unforgiving, and grout lines make the surface somewhat irregular. The result is that glasses tip easily and are more likely to break on the hard tiles. A tile surface is extremely durable, but if a tile should become damaged it can be replaced without tearing out the whole counter. Prices vary based on the type of tile.

**Natural stone** counters can be installed as a slab or as individual tiles. Stone comes in a beautiful array of colors, from dark-flecked granite *(pictured above)* and gray soapstone to white marble and pale, mottled limestone *(pictured above)*. Overall, stone is extremely durable and resistant to heat, but like tile it can be tough on delicate glassware. Most stone should be treated with a sealer to prevent stains (soapstone is an exception). Limestone and some light-colored marbles will not keep their pristine surface, even after sealing, and may stain over time. If possible, try to see a stone counter that's been in place for a few years and compare it with what you see in the showroom. Stone is a relatively expensive option.

**Wood** has been supplanted as a countertop material in many homes by a host of newer materials that require less maintenance. Yet it remains a naturally warm and attractive material that can be protected from water with a sealer. Butcher block made from rock maple *(pictured above)* is a frequent choice, but counters are fashioned from just about any kind of wood. Prices vary with the type of wood, but it can be an economical option.

**Solid-surface** countertops are practical: easy to clean, easy to repair, and available in many colors and patterns. They also can be combined with an integral sink of the same material. More gentle on plates and glasses than either stone or tile, they also don't stain easily, if at all. Known widely as Corian (which is made by DuPont), solid surfaces are also manufactured by a number of other companies. These countertops are moderately expensive.

**Concrete** is currently a popular choice for countertops. Because it can be formed into virtually any shape or thickness and enlivened with almost any kind of inlay,

face-frame cabinets

frameless cabinets

laminate cabinets

cherry wood cabinets

concrete offers unrivaled design possibilities. It can be cast in place or in a fabricator's shop and then installed like a stone slab. Like tile and stone, concrete is an unforgiving surface and will absorb stains if left unsealed. Concrete tends to be a relatively expensive installation.

**Stone composites,** such as Silestone and Zodiac, are blends of mostly real stone and a resin binder along with pigments for color. They are more uniform and predictable than natural stone and slightly less expensive. Quartz composites are very tough and, unlike real stone, won't absorb stains. Stone composite countertops are easy to maintain.

## Kitchen and Bath Cabinets

### Types of Cabinetry

Kitchen and bath cabinets are available in just about any architectural style and price range. Whether you're looking for a distressed antique finish, easy-to-clean laminate, or natural wood, you should be able to find just what you want. The most economical cabinet lines – what the cabinet industry calls "stock" – have the most limited choices in finish, materials, and hardware. Semi-custom cabinets offer more diverse finishes as well as superior materials and construction (dovetailed solid wood drawers, for example, rather than hardboard). Both stock and semi-custom lines are built in increments of 3" (7.5 cm), so filler strips are used to fit them to a room that doesn't fall exactly on that grid. At the top end are fully custom cabinets, built to any size

and with virtually any material. Because custom cabinets are made to order, be prepared to wait awhile to get them, and prices can be steep.

**Face-frame cabinets** *(pictured above)* are traditional in appearance, thanks to a wood frame applied to the face of the cabinet box that creates openings for drawers and doors. Depending on the look you want, face-frame cabinets can be ordered with inset or overlay doors and drawers, and with exposed or hidden door hardware. Cabinets can be ordered in many natural woods, including cherry, oak, and maple, with a variety of stains, or with painted or glazed surfaces.

**Frameless cabinets** *(pictured above),* a construction technique that originated in post-war Europe, are more contemporary in appearance than face-frame cabinets. Doors and drawer fronts cover the front of cabinet boxes completely, so all you see are the narrow gaps between doors and drawers. Frameless cabinets have a little more room inside because there's no overhanging face frame, and changing the entire look of the kitchen is as simple as buying new doors and drawer fronts.

### Cabinetry Materials

**Melamine** is one of the most economical materials available for cabinet construction. It consists of particleboard topped by a thin layer of plastic resin. High-pressure laminate *(pictured above),* the same material that's used to make kitchen countertops, is also used as a finish material in cabinet construction. Of the two, laminate is more durable, but both are available in many colors and are easy to keep clean because they won't

absorb spills. One disadvantage, especially with melamine, is that the surface is difficult to repair if it chips. On laminate doors, the dark lines along seams and edges can be concealed with PVC tape or by using color-through laminate.

**Thermofoil doors and drawers** are made to look like painted wood, but they are actually plastic that's formed around a core of medium-density fiberboard. Because the fiberboard takes such crisp detailing, you can get the look of a traditional raised panel door or drawer in an easy-care material and at a lower cost. A thermofoil door doesn't have as many seams as one made from high-pressure laminate, which means fewer places where seams could separate, but thermofoil isn't as heat tolerant.

**Wood cabinets** have a warmth and character that no manmade material can duplicate completely. Hardwoods and veneers such as oak, maple, cherry *(pictured above),* and alder are available from many manufacturers and make durable, handsome cabinets. If your style is a little less traditional, there are many other species to choose from – Douglas fir, quarter-sawn white oak, antique heart pine, and mahogany, for example. Keep in mind, though, that the more exotic the wood, the more it will cost.

**Finishes for natural wood cabinets** run the gamut, from crystal clear varnish to color-tinted lacquer and sophisticated marriages of glaze and stain. While wood can be stained to just about any shade, you can also rely more on wood's natural appearance by working from a basic palette of textures and colors – think

blond maple versus a dark ruby cherry. In addition to offering clear-coat finishes, manufacturers in recent years have broadened their offerings of glazes. These more complex surfaces include a second color layer that is applied and then mostly, but not completely, wiped away. The process leaves vestiges of color in corners and along moulding profiles. If you like the look of age, choose cabinets whose finishes have been intentionally distressed or sanded through at the factory. These finishes mimic the effects of many years of use, exactly the right effect in a renovated country kitchen.

### Redecorating Cabinets

Paint applied by brush or spray gun is a simple way of coaxing new life out of old kitchen cabinets without much expense, as long as the cabinets are structurally sound. Finishes won't be quite as durable as those applied in the factory to new cabinetry, so expect to touch up chips and nicks periodically (make sure the painter leaves some paint behind). Replacing hardware at the same time completes the makeover.

Re-facing cabinets with wood and adding new drawer fronts and doors is another way of reviving a tired kitchen. It's almost always less expensive than tearing out old cabinets and replacing them, and the process usually takes only a few days. Lots of wood species are available. Specialized fabricators make doors and drawer fronts in their shops, and veneer components like cabinet boxes right in your kitchen. New hardware completes the transformation.

claw-foot bathtub

tub with concrete surround and faucet

glass-door ceramic tile shower

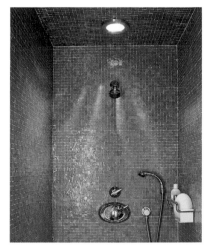

glass mosaic tile shower

## Bathtubs

**Porcelain enamel over cast iron** makes an extremely durable tub. Claw-foot tubs *(pictured above)* have a vintage look that's prized today. They are available new, and old ones can still be found in salvage yards, proof of just how long they hold up. These tubs get their long life from the process by which they're made: an enamel mixture is sprayed onto a molded cast-iron core and the tub is fired at a high temperature, fusing the two materials and creating a stain-resistant, easy-to-clean surface. Be careful not to use abrasive cleaners, which can damage the surface. Filled with warm water, cast-iron tubs are good at retaining heat for a long soak.

**Enameled steel** is a low-cost alternative to porcelain enamel over cast iron. These tubs are also lighter in weight, so they won't dampen the sound of running water or hold heat quite as effectively as cast iron. Although economy steel tubs are not as durable as cast iron, some higher-priced versions combine alloy steel with a structural composite underneath for longer life and better insulation qualities.

**Gelcoat tubs,** among the most economical options, are made by spraying a smooth resin coating on a mold and reinforcing the back with fiberglass and resin. The thin outer layer of a gelcoat tub is not as durable as other materials, and the finish can be damaged by careless cleaning. Still, gelcoat may be a good choice in a bathroom that isn't used every day, like a vacation home or guest bath.

**Acrylic tubs** are more durable and scratch resistant than gelcoat fixtures, and come with a proportionally higher price. The outer color layer is thicker, which helps the tub last longer. Like gelcoat tubs, the shells of acrylic tubs are reinforced with another material for strength.

**Replacement tub liners** made from acrylic plastic can save the trouble and expense of tearing out and replacing a tub that's seen better days. After taking measurements and ordering components, a contractor returns to install the new tub and shower walls in about a day. Although the process is not inexpensive, it's less costly than hiring a remodeling contractor, buying a new tub, and waiting for the work to be finished.

**Old bathtubs** stained and chipped from decades of use can be refinished on-site. Technicians thoroughly clean the surface, fill chips and scratches, and apply a new topcoat. A sprayed acrylic, which takes about a day to cure, can have either a matte or gloss finish. Many specialized contractors offer the service. Pristine white again, the acrylic surface will have a plastic quality that the original enamel didn't. Try to see samples of the coating or a refinished tub before you commit.

### Specialty Bathtubs

**Soaking tubs** are a long-standing tradition in Japan that for good reason is gaining popularity worldwide. Few things are as thoroughly relaxing as sitting in hot, chin-deep water at the end of the day. Ranging from 20" (51 cm) to as deep as 36" (90 cm), soaking tubs are much deeper than standard tubs and are a big part of the trend toward freestanding tubs in today's bathrooms. Extra-tall tubs can be hard to get into; you may need a wide, sturdy stepstool to help. Something else to

keep in mind: as tubs get deeper and hold more water, their weight increases. A 32"-deep (81 cm) tub may hold 60–75 gallons (227–284 l) of water, a potential strain on floor framing as well as a standard-capacity hot-water heater.

**Whirlpool tubs** add jets of water to the bath for an aquatic massage that can be adjusted in intensity. Whirlpools are considerably more expensive than standard tubs, but they ease tired muscles at the end of a long day, and some can accommodate more than one person. Very large tubs hold 150 gallons (568 l) or more of water and may require special floor framing for support as well as dedicated hot-water equipment.

**Air-jet tubs** use streams of bubbles rather than jets of water to relax the bather. Because they don't recirculate bath water through an internal network of pipes, they require less maintenance than a whirlpool. They are also somewhat less expensive than the most elaborate whirlpools.

## Showers

**Custom tile showers** *(pictured above)* provide unrivaled design possibilities. Shower pans made on-site with a mortar bed can be constructed in any size and shape, and a truly vast selection of ceramic and stone tile offers colors, textures, and patterns to suit any taste. Tile showers can be designed so they don't need a door, and they may be sunlit by glass-block windows or walls. Many kinds of ceramic and stone tile can be used, but stay away from smooth, highly polished surfaces on the floor, as they can be slippery. Shower tiles can be specified in smaller sizes to prevent slipping.

**One-piece tub/shower combination units** are available in gelcoat fiberglass or acrylic. Fully enclosed acrylic tub/showers with integral ceilings can be fitted with steam generators or elaborate multihead showers. Because of their size, one-piece tub/showers may not fit through halls and doorways during a renovation, but manufacturers also offer two- and three-piece models that can be negotiated into a bathroom more easily.

**Standalone** manufactured showers fit in smaller spaces than a combination tub/shower. There is a considerable range of designs and cost, including acrylic and fiberglass models that fit snugly into a corner and those with curved or angled faces. Larger units may include features such as molded seats, adjustable showerheads, and built-in wall niches.

## Toilets

Toilets come in a variety of styles and price ranges, but by government regulation they are now required to use no more than 1.6 gallons (6 l) of water per flush – a far cry from the 3–5 gallons (11–19 l) that older toilets typically used. Floor-mounted toilets are the most common type, but wall-mounted models also are available. They free up more floor space, making the bathroom look bigger, and they also make cleaning more convenient. Taller-than-average models better accommodate the needs of someone who uses a wheelchair or who has trouble sitting down and standing up.

There are two basic toilet designs. By far the most common are the gravity-feed designs. They release the contents of a

teak

painted wicker

powder-coated aluminum

cotton matelassé

water tank when the flush valve is opened and rely on gravity and the weight of water to do the rest. Pressure-assist toilets tap the pressure in the household plumbing system or use a pump to help expel waste. In some models, water consumption is less than the 1.6-gallon (6 l) standard. Power-assist models provide a forceful flushing action, but they're typically more expensive and noisier.

**Two-piece toilets** consist of a bowl and a separate water tank that are connected by the plumber at the time of installation. Some models are specially designed for corner installations, and those old-fashioned toilets with the tank mounted high on the wall are still available.

**One-piece toilets**, which tend to be more expensive, have fewer crevices and seams than two-piece designs. They look more contemporary and are easier to clean.

## Outdoor Furniture

**Teak** *(pictured above)* is the benchmark for outdoor wooden furniture: beautiful, long-lasting, and virtually maintenance-free. The luxuriant brown color of this tropical hardwood fades to a silver-gray over time, yet the oil-rich wood needs only an occasional scrubbing to maintain its subdued good looks.

**Mahogany** is a long-standing favorite, in part because of the wood's high rot resistance and its deep reddish-brown color. Long a favorite of boat builders, mahogany was the material used in the original deck chairs on the *Titanic* (a Nantucket, Massachusetts, company produces a line of reproduction deck

chairs based on one salvaged at the scene of the 1912 North Atlantic wreck). The wood weathers naturally to a soft gray.

**A variety of tropical hardwoods,** such as ipé, jarrah, balau, and nyatoh, are alternatives to the better-known teak and mahogany. Prices should be less than what you'd pay for top grades of teak, but these woods also are strong, dense, and weather resistant. Reddish-brown colors fade to an attractive silver-gray with exposure to sun and rain, but an application of oil can restore the original color.

**Cedar and redwood** are alternatives to imported tropical hardwoods. Both of these North American softwoods have long histories as durable outdoor building materials with excellent resistance to rot and insects. Clear, tight-grained heartwood promises the best weather resistance, but supplies are dwindling. Neither of these woods is as dense as the tropical hardwoods, making them a little more susceptible to wear and tear. And unlike the tropicals, they need periodic applications of wood preservative.

**Wicker** furniture *(pictured above)* is generally woven from flexible branches or twigs. Synthetic fibers are now being used to create wicker for all-weather outdoor use. Unlike natural wicker furniture, all-season versions are woven over frames of aluminum or plastic and can be left out in the rain, even snow, with little or no ill effect. Best of all, they have all the comfort and charm of the real thing.

**Rattan, water hyacinth, seagrass, and abaca** are all plant fibers used to make attractive woven furniture with a natural outdoors look. These fibers can be dyed,

but they're not intended to be left outside. Count on protecting them from sun and rain under a patio or porch roof.

**Cast iron and wrought iron** are timeless choices for patio and garden furniture, and they won't get blown around in a storm. Metal can be formed into just about any shape, opening the door to ornate furniture designs that aren't possible with other materials. Iron rusts when exposed to water, so it must be painted (and repainted periodically) to protect it. Alternately, some manufacturers apply a plastic-like coating to ward off corrosion.

**Aluminum** is the most widely used material for outdoor furniture today, and it has one big advantage over iron: it won't rust. But, left unprotected, aluminum will pit and oxidize in the weather, so look for furniture that has a protective powder-coated finish *(pictured above)*. Outdoor aluminum furniture comes in a variety of grades. Hollow tubular furniture is the most economical choice and offers lightweight portability. Furniture made from cast aluminum components is heavier, sturdier, and available in many styles and finishes, though top grades can be quite expensive.

**Plastic** makes an inexpensive and durable material that can be molded into a variety of striking shapes for outdoor furniture. Armed with UV inhibitors, plastic is impervious to the weather and available in bright colors. If you're looking for the advantages of plastic in more traditional styles, there's now furniture made from recycled plastic that looks like painted wood. Adirondack-style chairs and rockers are among the offerings.

**Weather-resistant cushions and fabrics** add a burst of color and texture to metal and wood furniture, and make a long Sunday afternoon lounge a lot more comfortable. Plain cotton canvas that had to be raced inside during a rainstorm has given way to much hardier synthetic materials that look great, resist fading, and are easier to clean. Weather-treated canvas is also available.

## Fabrics

**Canvas** is a heavy-duty fabric commonly used to make sporting goods, awnings, and tents. Woven from cotton, linen, or hemp, canvas has a casual, relaxed appearance and can be used inside or out for upholstery and pillows. It's an excellent choice for outdoor furniture cushions; look for canvas that has been treated with Teflon to repel water and resist sun fading.

**Chenille** weaves silk, cotton, or synthetic fibers into tufted cords to create a fabric of great depth and richness. Aptly named after the French word for "caterpillar," this luxuriously furry material is used to make blankets, throws, and furniture upholstery.

**Cotton** is a lightweight fabric woven from spun fibers from the boll of the cotton plant. Breathable, washable, and endlessly versatile, it's the perfect all-season fabric for bedding, upholstery, and window coverings. Long-staple or Egyptian cottons are the softest options for bedding, while sun-treated canvas and twills are durable choices for outdoor furnishings. Cotton is often blended with linen, wool, silk, or synthetic fibers.

raw linen

twill

sisal rug

kilim rug

**Denim** is a heavy, twill-woven cotton fabric that is believed to have originated in France and was popularized in the United States during the California Gold Rush in the form of work pants (jeans). Denim is a great washable slipcover option for casual rooms, especially where children and pets play, as well as outdoor rooms. Repeated washings soften the fabric, adding to its appeal.

**Faux suede** is designed to mimic the look and touch of genuine napped leather. Made of microfibers, this durable synthetic offers a soft, washable upholstery option for sofas and chairs and contributes a lush feeling to rooms.

**Leather** makes an exceptionally durable upholstery option that gets more supple and beautiful with age. The surface texture, dimension, pigment regularity, and softness of the tanned hide all distinguish high-quality leather. Black and brown are classic leather colors, but manufacturers now dye leathers in a range of attractive hues. Leather furnishings suit both contemporary and classic interiors.

**Linen** *(pictured above)* is woven from the fibers of the flax plant. Twice as strong as cotton, this crisp, breathable fabric has a naturally nubby texture that softens with use. Linen is a popular choice for tablecloths and napkins, draperies, and upholstery. It is often blended with cotton for easier care. Machine-washable linens are now widely available.

**Matelassé** *(pictured above)* is a double-woven fabric, usually of cotton, with raised decorative patterns that mimic the look of a quilt (*matelassé* means "cushioned" in French). In fact, the effect is achieved through the process

of weaving in an interlocking wadding weft (a filled thread or yarn) rather than through quilting. Matelassé bedding, pillows, and throws lend rich texture and vintage appeal to a room.

**Silk** is woven from threads unwound from cocoons of the Japanese silkworm. Prized for its beautiful sheen and smooth texture, silk is a luxurious option for draperies and pillow coverings.

**Synthetic fibers** such as rayon, polyester, nylon, and acrylic are woven into a wide range of natural fabrics to make them more durable and easier to maintain.

**Terry cloth**, the classic toweling fabric, is usually woven of cotton and has a looped surface that is naturally absorbent. Because it washes well, dries fast, and withstands humidity, terry makes an ideal upholstery fabric or pillow covering for bathrooms and outdoor spaces.

**Twill** *(pictured above)* is a cotton fabric that is tightly woven with a raised diagonal grain. Denim and gabardine are examples of twill weaves. Durable, washable, and comfortable, cotton twill is a hardworking choice for slipcovers or upholstery, indoors and out. Sun-treated twills stand up to outdoor use best.

**Velvet** is traditionally woven from wool, silk, or cotton. Its raised pile consists of rows of loops that are cut to produce a plush, fur-like texture. A classic choice for draperies and upholstery, velvet brings a rich and elegant accent to interiors.

**Wool** makes a naturally strong, warm, and resilient fabric for home furnishings. Wool fibers are commonly blended with natural fibers or synthetics.

## Rugs

**Abaca**, also called Manila hemp, is an extremely strong fiber that comes from the leafstalk of a banana plant that is native to the Philippines. Abaca is not related to true hemp, although both are used to make twine, fabric, and rugs.

**Coir** is a natural fiber derived from coconut husks. Once removed from the husks, the fiber is spun and machine woven into matting. Coir mats have a coarse finish and are generally considered the toughest of the natural-fiber rugs. Coir is a good option for entryways and hallways and is widely used for doormats.

**Cotton** yarns are woven to make rugs that feel soft and springy underfoot, with the added advantage of being easy to clean. Styles range from the tapestry-weave dhurries of India to American designs such as braided rugs and rag rugs. Naturally absorbent, cotton mats are the rug of choice for bathrooms.

**Jute** comes from a strong, woody plant grown extensively in Asia. When woven into matting, it has a lush appearance and texture akin to wool. Jute is considered the softest underfoot of the natural woven mats, but in general does not prove as long-wearing as sisal or seagrass.

**Paper** rugs are woven from fibers extracted from wood pulp. Surprisingly durable and comfortable underfoot, paper rugs are woven in attractive patterns that have the look of sisal and other natural matting. They are an environmentally sound option, as wood is recyclable and biodegradable.

**Seagrass** is a commercially grown aquatic grass from China that produces a fiber similar to straw and smoother than coir, sisal, or jute. It is naturally resistant to dirt and stains, making it suitable for higher-traffic areas. The subtle green tones of seagrass (which eventually soften to brown) add warmth and outdoor appeal to a room.

**Sisal** *(pictured above)* is a flexible fiber made from the leaves of the sisal (or agave) plant, which grows in Asia, Africa, and Central America. Sisal fibers are woven into hardwearing rugs with an even, highly textural surface. Sisal rugs are relatively soft, making them a fine choice for living areas and bedrooms. Their durability also makes them suitable for entryways and hallways.

**Synthetic** rugs — machine-woven of fibers such as nylon, rayon, polyester, or acrylic — are durable, stain resistant, and affordable. Polypropylene is a petroleum-based synthetic that can be woven into striking patterns that look like natural sisal or wool. Easy to clean with water, polypropylene rugs are a practical choice in high-traffic rooms such as entries and kitchens and in outdoor areas.

**Wool** rugs are naturally warm, water repellent, and long-lasting. Most wool carpets are woven with synthetic fibers, typically in a blend of 80 percent wool, 20 percent nylon. Wool yarns are traditionally used to weave intricately patterned Oriental and Tibetan rugs as well as the kilims of Turkey and Afghanistan *(pictured above)*.

# Index

# Acknowledgments

## PRINCIPAL PHOTOGRAPHERS

HOTZE EISMA Pages 21, 44 (bottom left), 53 (middle right), 198–201, 206 (top left and right, bottom right), 208–17, 218 (top left, bottom right), 222–27, 229 (top left, bottom), 230 (bottom left and right), 232–35, 236, 237 (top left and right, middle left, bottom). Following images © Hotze Eisma: 136 (bottom left), 142–43, 148–49, 153 (bottom right), 155, 160–61.

JIM FRANCO Pages 2–6, 10–11, 14, 17, 42 (top left), 43, 46–47, 54–55 (center), 55 (top), 74, 75 (top), 80–81, 96 (top), 100 (top right), 108 (top left and right), 110 (top left), 128, 136 (top left), 138–39, 162–63 (center), 163–65, 189 (top left and center), 220–21, 228, 268–69, 302–03, 328, 332 (bottom), 333, 334–35, 354–55, 306, 318, 332 (top), 356, 358 (second and third from left), 360 (first from left), 361 (first, third, and fourth from left).

MARK LUND Back cover (bottom left); pages 52 (bottom), 53 (top right), 54, 180 (top), 238–41, 246 (top right, bottom left, bottom right), 248–54, 258–59, 260 (bottom), 260–61 (center), 261 (top), 262–67, 276 (bottom right), 282 (top left and right, bottom left), 284–85, 288–89, 316 (top), 322 (bottom), 346, 348 (bottom), 352 (bottom).

STEFANO MASSEI Pages 32 (top left), 42 (top right), 53 (middle left, bottom left and right), 55 (bottom), 68 (top), 116, 117 (top right, bottom left), 136 (top right, bottom right), 144 (top left and right, bottom left), 150–51, 152 (bottom), 153 (top right), 154, 159, 162 (top), 176–77, 180 (bottom), 181 (bottom right), 182 (top left, bottom right), 189 (top right), 230 (top right), 260 (top), 261 (bottom), 276 (top left and right, bottom left), 278–81, 312 (bottom), 327 (top), 358 (fourth from left), 359 (third from left), 360 (second from left).

DAVID MATHESON Front cover (top right), front flap (bottom), back cover (top left, bottom right), back flap (top); pages 16 (left), 19, 41 (bottom left), 62–67, 78–79, 83–95, 96 (bottom), 97 (top left and right, bottom right), 98 (top left), 99, 100 (top left, bottom left and right), 102–07, 108 (bottom), 109, 110 (top right, bottom left and right), 112–15, 117 (top left, middle left, bottom right), 118, 120–27, 130, 140–41, 144 (bottom right), 146 47, 153 (top left), 156, 158, 162 (bottom), 172 (top left), 190 (top left), 229 (top right), 230 (top left), 271, 282 (bottom right), 290–301, 308, 311, 315, 321, 324, 352 (top), 359 (second and fourth from left). Following image © David Matheson: page 98 (middle left).

PRUE RUSCOE Front flap (top); pages 8–9, 32 (top right), 41 (bottom right), 56 (top right, bottom left), 58 (bottom), 167, 172 (top right, bottom left and right), 174–75, 178–79, 181 (top right and left, middle right and left), 182 (top right, bottom left), 184–88, 189 (bottom), 190 (top right, bottom left and right), 192–97, 206 (bottom left), 246 (top left), 305, 313, 342, 344–45.

ALAN WILLIAMS Back cover (top right), back flap (bottom); pages 1, 13, 18, 20, 22 (left), 23–27, 32 (bottom right and left), 34–38, 39 (top), 40, 41 (top right, middle right and left), 42 (bottom), 44 (top right and left, bottom right), 48–51, 52 (top), 53 (top left), 56 (top left, bottom right), 58 (top, middle), 58–59, 60–61, 69 (middle right, bottom right), 70–73, 74–75 (center), 75 (bottom), 76–77, 97 (bottom left), 117 (middle right), 218 (top right, bottom left), 256–57, 312 (top), 316, 317 (bottom), 322 (top), 323, 326, 327 (bottom), 337, 338, 340, 348 (top), 349, 350, 352, 358 (first from left), 359 (first from left).

## ADDITIONAL PHOTOGRAPHERS

MELANIE ACEVEDO Front flap (top); page 16 (right), 286–87. DAN CLARK Pages 41 (top left), 68 (bottom), 69 (top left, top right, middle right, bottom left), 152 (top), 237 (middle right), 361 (second from left). Following images © REED DAVIS: front cover (top left, bottom right). Following image © DANA GALLAGHER: page 98 (middle right). Following image © ALEC HEMER: page 22 (right). Following image © MAURA MCEVOY: page 181 (bottom left). Following image © DAVID TSAY: page 39 (bottom left). Following images © ANNA WILLIAMS: Page 98 (bottom left, bottom right).

## ADDITIONAL IMAGES

© ANN SACKS TILE Page 68 (bottom box upper right, lower left and right). © ARMSTRONG HARDWOOD FLOORING BY HARTCO Page 357 (top left). © ARMSTRONG LAMINATE FLOORING Page 357 (second from left). © BEATE WORKS, INC Page 153 (bottom left). © ECOTIMBER Page 357 (top right). © ROBBINS FINE HARDWOOD FLOORING FROM ARMSTRONG Page 357 (third from left). © SCAVOLINI Page 360 (third and fourth from left).

## PRINCIPAL STYLISTS

ANTHONY ALBERTUS Front cover (bottom left); pages 16 (right), 21, 53 (middle right), 98 (middle right), 198–99, 201, 206 (top left and right, bottom right), 208–18, 222–27, 229 (top left, bottom), 230 (bottom left and right), 232–35, 236–37, 286–87, 306, 318, 332 (top), 356, 358 (second and third from left), 360 (first from left), 361 (first, third, and fourth from left).

NADINE BUSH Front cover (top right), front flap (bottom), back cover (bottom right); pages 16 (left), 62 (bottom left), 83, 89–95, 96 (bottom), 97 (top left and right, bottom right), 98 (top left), 99, 100 (top left, bottom right), 102–07, 110 (top right, bottom left and right), 112–15, 117 (top left, middle left, bottom right), 118 (top right, bottom left), 122–23, 126–27, 130, 140–41, 144 (bottom right), 146–47, 153 (top left), 156, 158, 172 (top left), 308, 352 (top), 359 (second and fourth from left).

DEBORAH MCLEAN Pages 24–25, 38 (top), 39 (top), 41 (middle left), 50–51, 58 (top, middle), 58–59, 68 (top), 70 (bottom left), 75 (bottom), 116, 117 (bottom left), 144 (top right and left, bottom left), 154, 159, 162 (top), 180 (bottom), 182 (top left, bottom right), 189 (top right), 230 (top right), 260 (top), 261 (bottom), 276 (top left), 278–81, 316 (bottom), 327 (bottom), 340, 358 (fourth from left).

EDWARD PETERSON Front flap (top); pages 8–9, 32 (top right), 41 (bottom right), 56 (top right, bottom left), 58 (bottom), 98 (middle left, bottom right), 167, 172 (top right, bottom left), 174–75, 178–79, 181 (top left and right, middle left and right), 182 (top right, bottom left), 184–88, 189 (bottom), 190 (top right, bottom left and right), 192–97, 206 (bottom left), 246 (top left), 305, 313, 342, 344–45.

ALISTAIR TURNBULL Pages 42 (top right), 53 (middle left, bottom right), 55 (bottom), 117 (top right), 136 (top right, bottom right), 150–51, 152 (bottom), 153 (top right), 176–77, 181 (bottom right), 276 (top right, bottom left), 312 (bottom), 327 (top), 359 (third from left).

MICHAEL WALTERS Back cover (top left and right, bottom left), back flap (bottom); pages 1–6, 10–14, 17–20, 22 (right), 23, 27, 32 (bottom left and right), 35–37, 38 (bottom), 40, 41 (top right, middle right, bottom left), 42 (top left, bottom), 43, 44 (top right and left, bottom right), 46–49, 52, 53 (top left and right), 54, 54–55 (center), 55 (top), 56 (top left, bottom right), 60–61, 61, 62 (top right, bottom right), 64–67, 69 (middle right, bottom right), 70 (top left and right, bottom right), 72–74, 74–75 (center), 75 (top), 76–81, 96 (top), 97 (bottom left), 100 (top right), 108 (top left and right), 110 (top left), 117 (middle right), 118 (top left, bottom right), 120–21, 124–25, 127, 128, 136 (top left), 138–39, 162 (bottom), 162–163 (center), 163–65, 180 (top), 189 (top left, center), 190 (top left), 220–21, 228, 238–41, 246 (top right, bottom left and right), 248–50, 251 (top right, middle, bottom), 252–59, 260 (bottom), 260–61 (center), 261 (top), 262–71, 276 (bottom right), 282, 284–85, 288–301, 302–03, 310, 312 (top), 315, 316, 317 (top), 320, 322–23, 325, 326, 328, 332 (bottom), 333, 334–35, 337, 338, 346, 348–49, 350, 352 (bottom), 353, 354–55, 358 (first from left), 359 (first from left).

## ADDITIONAL STYLISTS

DAVID BENRUD Page 22 (left). JULIA BIRD Pages 160-161. PHILLIPPA BRAITHWAITE Page 98 (bottom left). HELEN CROWTHER Page 172 (bottom right). THEA GECK Pages 32 (top left), 53 (bottom left). GREG LOWE Page 251 (top left). MARY MULCAHY Front cover (top left, bottom right). CARLA ROLEY Page 44 (bottom left). NICOLE SILLAPERE Back flap (top), pages 100 (bottom left), 108 (bottom), 109, 229 (top right), 230 (top left).

## ILLUSTRATORS

SHANNON ABBEY Pages 28, 84, 132, 168, 202, 242, 272, 341, 343, 351.
NATE PADAVICK Pages 30–31, 39, 40, 86–87, 96, 99, 134–35, 155, 170–71, 204–05, 244–45, 274–75, 340, 342.

# Contributors

## PHOTOGRAPHERS

**HOTZE EISMA** is based in Amsterdam and has been shooting interiors for nearly 20 years. His work has appeared in numerous magazines round the world including *Condé Nast Traveler*, U.S. and European editions of *Elle Decoration*, and *Vogue Australia*. His other interior design books include *Pottery Barn Bathrooms*, *Contemporary Chic*, and *Simple Style*.

**JIM FRANCO** is a New York City–based lifestyle photographer. His clients include *Travel + Leisure*, *Condé Nast Traveller* UK, *Real Simple*, *Domino Magazine*, and Starwood Hotels.

**MARK LUND** lives in New York City. Born in Madison, Wisconsin, Mark was educated in both structural engineering and fine art, Mark photographed *Pottery Barn Workspaces*, and his work has appeared in numerous magazines including *Country Gardens*, *InStyle*, *O at Home*, *Real Simple*, and *Wired*.

**STEFANO MASSEI**, originally from Italy, is now based in San Francisco. His work has appeared in international magazines including *Abitare*, *Elle Decoration Italia*, and *Parenting* as well as in print advertising, for clients including Arclinea, Fontana Arte, Gap, and Williams-Sonoma. Stefano also photographed *Pottery Barn Storage & Display*.

**DAVID MATHESON** is a freelance photographer based in Sydney, Australia. David photographed *Dining Spaces*, *Photos Style Recipes*, *Flowers Style Recipes*, and *Cocktails Style Recipes* for Pottery Barn's book series. He is a regular contributor to design magazines including *Vogue Entertaining + Travel* and *Gourmet Traveler*, and also photographed the acclaimed book *Patio* by Jamie Durie.

**PRUE RUSCOE** studied photography at Sydney College of the Arts and worked in fashion photography before establishing herself as a leading interiors and lifestyle photographer in Australia, the United States, and Europe. She photographed *Pottery Barn Bedrooms*, and her work has appeared in numerous publications including *Elle Decoration*, *Marie Claire Lifestyle*, *Vogue Entertaining & Travel*, and *Vogue Living*. Prue is based in Sydney, Australia.

**ALAN WILLIAMS** has established a reputation as a leading photographer of architecture, interiors, and general lifestyle topics including travel, food, and drink. His previous books include *Pottery Barn Living Rooms*, *The Color Design Sourcebook*, and *Wine Tastes Wine Styles*. Born in Wales, Alan is now based in London, England.

## WRITERS

**KATHLEEN HACKETT ANTONSON** has written and edited more than 40 cooking and lifestyle books and wrote the text for *Pottery Barn Dining Spaces*. She is a former executive book editor for Martha Stewart Living Omnimedia.

**MARTHA FAY** has worked as a freelance writer for more than 20 years and is the author of two books of nonfiction. She writes frequently about design and was a contributor to *Pottery Barn Bedrooms*, *Storage & Display*, and *Workspaces*.

**SCOTT GIBSON** is a freelance writer and editor. A former staff editor at The Taunton Press, he writes for a number of publications including *Fine Woodworking*, *Fine Homebuilding*, *Inspired House*, and *Home*.

**CAROLE NICKSIN** has written for publications including the *New York Times*, *InStyle Home*, *Shop Etc.*, *Vitals*, *Home*, and *Martha Stewart Living*.

**MARILYN ZELINSKY-SYARTO** has edited design and architecture books, authored three books on the evolving workplace, and written dozens of articles on home design and products.

## WELDON OWEN WISHES TO THANK

Birdman, Inc.; Darrell Coughlan, merchandise coordinator; Ken DellaPenta, indexer; Wim de Vos, architect; Sherreme Gurtler, stylist assistant; Kathy Kaiser, copyeditor; Kass Kapsiak, caterer; Deborah Kirk, development consultant; Jean Larette, interior design consultant; Sean MacDonald, merchandise coordinator; Jim Pfaffman, architectural consultant; John Robbins, photography assistant; Peter Scott; Kimball Stone, merchandise coordinator; Daniel Weiner, photography assistant. Thanks to Joyce Robertson and Lost Arts, San Francisco; the Pottery Barn product development team; and the staff at the Pottery Barn store, Corte Madera, California, for supplying props and artwork.

Many thanks also to everyone who has contributed to the Pottery Barn publishing program, including Leonie Barrera, Joseph DeLeo, Elizabeth Dougherty, Elizabeth Lazich, Tim Lewis, Lisa Light, Sarah Lynch, Jackie Mancuso, Gina Risso, Mario Serafin, Allison Serrell, Forrest Stilin, Colin Wheatland, and Joshua Young. Special thanks to Shawna Mullen for her initial work on the development of this book.

## ABOUT POTTERY BARN

Pottery Barn is America's leading source for furniture, accessories, and inspiration. Since the company's inception in 1949 as a single store in lower Manhattan, Pottery Barn has brought its signature blend of comfort and style to homes across America. For more about Pottery Barn, visit www.potterybarn.com.